THE TWELVE
WHO WALKED
IN GALILEE

Woodrow W. Smith

THE TWELVE WHO WALKED IN GALILEE

Character Studies of the Members of Jesus' Cabinet

FLEMING H. REVELL COMPANY
Old Tappan, New Jersey

Unless otherwise identified, all Scripture quotations are from the Revised Standard Version of the Bible, copyrighted 1946 and 1952.

Scripture quotations marked KJV are from the King James Version of the Bible.

Scripture quotations marked NEB are from The New English Bible. © The Delegates of the Oxford University Press and the Syndics of the Cambridge University Press 1961 and 1970. Reprinted by permission.

"The Song of a Heathen" by Richard Watson Gilder from COLLECTED WORKS OF RICHARD WATSON GILDER, published by Houghton Mifflin Company. Used by permission.

"Thomas" by Eutychas. Copyright 1962 by Christianity Today; used by permission.

"God has put a value on the soul" by Ben F. Lehmberg in *Food for Tasting*, 1969, published by Tidings Press is used by permission.

Excerpt from THE GREAT MAZE AND THE HEART OF YOUTH by Hermann Hagedorn. Used by permission.

Excerpt from THOUGHTS AFIELD by Harold Kohn. Published by Wm. B. Eerdmans Publishing Co. and used by permission.

Scripture quotations marked TEV are from the Today's English Version of the New Testament. Copyright © American Bible Society 1966.

Library of Congress Cataloging in Publication Data

Smith, Woodrow W
    The twelve who walked in Galilee.

    Bibliography: p.
    1. Apostles. I. Title.
BS2440.S55   225.9′2 [B]   73-16410
ISBN 0-8007-0636-6

TO

Dr. J. Kenneth Shamblin
whose confidence in me is a constant source of strength and
   encouragement
whose commitment to the Christian life is an inspiration
whose friendship is treasured

Contents

I. THE PROLOGUE

II. JESUS' CABINET

III. THE EPILOGUE

Preface

Dr. Earl Marlatt, one of my favorite professors at Perkins School of Theology, often told his students, "You are not all of yourself; your friends are the rest of you." He was saying that intimacy with and confidence in other persons is risky business, that friendship can either support life's highest values or destroy them, strengthen character or weaken it. Hence, the importance of selectivity in all human relationships.

One of the finest experiences of my life has been my association with the twelve men who walked with Jesus in Galilee. Through the disciplines of study and preaching I came to know them as real persons, and to appreciate them as men of courage and commitment. They have won a large place in my heart and their influence has contributed immeasurably to the development of my life and ministry. They have helped me to understand the gospel more fully, have caused me to deepen my commitment to the living of the Christian life, and have made me want to fulfill more adequately my responsibility as a Methodist preacher. Today I am not all of myself. These twelve men have become a part of me and I am a better person because of their friendship.

If reading this book enables you to experience something of the warmth and genuineness of this friendship then my efforts will not have been in vain. My prayer is that this adventure in discovery will enrich your life and strengthen your Christian commitments.

I wish to express my appreciation to the good people of Grand Avenue Methodist Church, Hot Springs, Arkansas, who first heard these messages from the pulpit and for their encouragement to put them in written form.

I am deeply indebted to Dr. J. Kenneth Shamblin and Dr. Charles L. Allen for their confidence in me and for their belief in the value of this book. Without their help these chapters never would have been published.

Special thanks is due Mrs. Pat Parker, Mrs. Philip Liberto, and Mrs. Wayne Shively who typed the manuscript in its various stages of development.

Finally, a word of high appreciation to my wife, Betty, and our four wonderful children—Cheryl, Pamela, Jerry, and Donnie—for they are the dearest people in my life. Their patience with me and their support of my commitment to the Christian ministry is like a deep reservoir from which I daily draw strength.

WOODROW W. SMITH

1

The Prologue

The best way of knowing God is to frequent
the company of His friends.

SAINT TERESA

They Gave Themselves to the Lord

Always a top news story is the selection of cabinet members by the president of the United States—men who then appear before the Senate Subcommittee seeking congressional approval.

In many ways their selection is reminiscent of a similar disclosure made over 1,950 years ago. Jesus had retreated to the mountains. A crowd followed Him. Then, according to Mark's interpretation, He appointed the Twelve—those who were to be His close traveling companions, His chief confidants, His dearest and most trusted friends. There were "Simon whom he surnamed Peter; James the son of Zebedee and John the brother of James . . . Andrew, and Philip, and Bartholomew, and Matthew, and Thomas, and James the son of Alphaeus, and Thaddaeus, and Simon the Cananaean, and Judas Iscariot, who betrayed him" (Mark 3:16–19). These were His disciples.

Like the cabinet members who serve under any administration, these disciples came from widely divergent backgrounds and represented a broad spectrum of experience. They accepted their posts at great sacrifice both to themselves and to their families. Entering public service plunged them into a life radically different from anything they had previously known—a life which was to bring them much personal abuse, harsh criticism, and at times severe persecution. Nevertheless, the disciples entered into their work joyously and with great expectation, proud of the chance to be of service to their Lord.

No doubt there are other similarities in the two cabinets, but there are also some striking differences. Whereas the president's chief advisors are well trained and highly qualified persons, Jesus' disciples were unlearned men and ill-prepared to undertake their respective missions. Instead of being assigned specific areas of responsibility, the disciples were given the same primary function, the sharing in and the proclamation of the good news of the gospel. The number of persons in Jesus' cabinet was chosen for symbolic rather than pragmatic reasons. There was one representative for each of the twelve tribes of Israel rather than one person to head each of the various divisions of government. Then, too, unlike the members of a presidential cabinet, the disciples had no budget, no staff to help them administer their work. Nor did their appointment require the confirmation of any organized body. If the disciples achieved any notoriety, it was not during their tenure of office, but long after they had passed from this temporal life. They were an ignominious group. Yet every Christian owes them an enormous debt of gratitude. Had it not been for the members of this cabinet our image of Jesus might have perished from human memory.

Following the events of that First Holy Week, the disciples chose not to remain in Jerusalem as an executive board, but to give themselves completely to the missionary cause. They wanted to answer the challenge of the great commission: "Go therefore and make disciples of all nations, baptizing them in the name of the Father and of the Son and of the Holy Spirit, teaching them to observe all that I have commanded you . . ." (Matthew 28:19, 20). There was no hesitation, no reluctance, only a passionate desire to bring men into a saving relationship with Jesus Christ. In this respect, they were truly dynamic disciples.

So we begin a provocative and stimulating adventure, one that will hopefully provide the reader with a clear understanding and a special appreciation of the members of Jesus' cabinet. The study is important because the disciples were the product of a great Teacher, the critical bridge between Jesus and the church, and because they provide the best examples of Christian discipleship.

First, the disciples were the product of a great Teacher. In many ways Jesus' cabinet was like a typical Sunday-school class — an especially rowdy one. Two of the Twelve wanted to have a fire bomb thrown into a crowd to get rid of the people they did not like (see Luke 9:51–55). Two others in the class persuaded their mother to try to inveigle some big honor for themselves from the Teacher (see Matthew 20:20, 21). One of the more lively members disgraced the others by blaspheming in public (see Matthew 26:69–75). Some had violent tempers and were prone to start class disputes (see Matthew 26:51; Mark 9:34; Luke 22:23). On at least one occasion three of them fell asleep when they should have been alert (see Matthew 26:40). It was not an easy class to teach, but Jesus handled the situation beautifully by practicing the finest principles of Christian education. Recognizing the limitations of the lecture method, He continually stirred the minds of His pupils with questions. My, how He delighted to engage the disciples in dialogue!

He knew that a picture is worth more than a thousand words. He expressed the sublimest truth in simple parables, and a parable is nothing more than a word picture. He was careful to take advantage of what educators call *the teachable moment,* and often went out of His way to create these precious opportunities for learning. He would take the disciples on quiet walks through the grain fields and the flower-bedecked meadows, or sit down and talk with them by some mountain stream.

He gave His students occasion for self-discovery by sending them out on preaching and healing missions. Jesus insisted the disciples learn by doing, by trial and error. In this respect, they all were graduated from the school of hard knocks.

He graded His teaching to the growth of individuals. One can almost hear Him say, "I have yet many things to say to you, but you cannot bear them now" (John 16:12). In other words, Jesus did not overload His class with assignments they were not ready to understand or experience.

Finally, and most important, He loved His students. He believed in them, had confidence in their ability, saw their potentialities and, by the sheer warmth of His personality, encouraged them to seek a higher and nobler plane of living. "Greater love has no man than this, that a man lay down his life for his friends. [He said,] . . . I have called you friends" (John 15:13, 15). It was this love that motivated the disciples to work with Him for the fulfillment of the Kingdom of God, that stimulated them to character development, and inspired them to achieve spiritual growth. Luke says the disciples learned so well that the world "took knowledge of them, that they had been with Jesus" (Acts 4:13 KJV).

W. O. Carrington, the gifted black poet-preacher, in a sermon entitled "Carry a Little Honey" says that we should not let die and be forgotten the beautiful parable of the ancient Persian poet and moralist, Saadi. In the legend, a piece of clay was asked if it were some rare or priceless perfume. The reply was that it was just a bit of common clay. When further pressed for the secret of its rare perfume, the clay modestly said, "I have companied all the summer with the rose." So the disciples—they were dynamic personalities not because of who they were but because of Him with whom they had associated. They were great not because of what had been taught them but because of Him at whose feet they had sat in the classroom of wisdom. The disciples were the product of a great Teacher.

They were also a critical bridge between the Master Teacher and the institutional church. It was their labor of love that gave both continuity and power to the rapidly expanding body of believers.

George Gipp, one of the greatest football players the game every knew, died at twenty-three years of age. He had been a rugged, hard-hitting player on one of Knute Rockne's Notre Dame teams and was affectionately known to his teammates and to football fans across the nation as "The Gipper." When death was near, Knute Rockne was called to the hospital to see Gipp. Fumbling for words to say to the dying boy, Rockne bent over him and said, "It's pretty tough to go, isn't it, Gipp?"

The boy smiled and answered, "What's tough about it? I've no complaints." Then he added, "Rock, I've got to go, and it's all right, and I'm not afraid. I'll plunge into this game of dying as I did into West Point and Southern California. Sometime, Rock, when the going is tough and everything goes wrong, and our team isn't getting a break, tell our boys to go in there with all they've got and win one game—just one game—for 'The Gipper.' Rock, I don't know exactly where I'll be, but I'll know about it. I'll be watching from somewhere, you can count on that."

Two years passed. Notre Dame's football team experienced a difficult season. Many boys suffered from injuries and the team's spirit was low. Then came the Army game, Gipp's favorite and the hardest contest of the year. At the end of the first half both teams were scoreless.

Between halves Knute Rockne talked quietly to the nearly demoralized team. He told them about his hospital call on George Gipp during the football hero's last days. He related to them the dying wish of the great athlete — "Win one game, just one, for 'The Gipper.'" The boys were hushed, reverent, and inwardly moved.

At the beginning of the last half, they ran out on the field and, as sports writers put it, "seemed inspired, exalted, overpowering." After a few minutes of play, with sweeping end runs and precise forward passes, Notre Dame was within striking distance of its goal. Chevigny was given the ball and bulldozed his way through Army for the winning touchdown. As Chevigny pawed his way out of the heap of players who had fallen over him, he smiled and said, "Boys, that's one for the old Gipper." Notre Dame had carried on for George Gipp.

Jesus' dying wish was that His death not be in vain, that His Kingdom not fail. He hoped and prayed that sometime, somehow, someone would come along, pick up the ball and carry it forward to victory. This is exactly what the members of His cabinet did. They were extensions of His spirit and power. They walked where His feet had never trod. They spoke His words in languages His lips never uttered. They used instruments of mercy His hands had never touched. They carried on for their Lord. The disciples were the living link between Christ and Christianity. Finally, they gave practical demonstration to the meaning of discipleship. Their commitment to Jesus' way of life is unmistakably plain in what they said and did.

One bitterly cold day during the American Revolution while the army was wintering at Valley Forge, a small group of soldiers was attempting to build a log hut. Their clothing was in tatters, their bleeding feet were wrapped in rags, they were weak from hunger and sickness, and their fingers were numb with cold. While they struggled to lift a heavy log into place, the officer in charge shouted orders and then cursed them for being unable to follow directions.

A tall dignified man in a dark cloak stopped to watch. After a few minutes, he turned to the officer. "That log could easily be placed in position with the help of one more man," he said.

"I know that," shouted the officer, "I've asked for more men, but headquarters won't give them to me."

"You might give a hand yourself," suggested the gentleman.

"Me?" sneered the officer. "Can't you see that I'm a corporal? I don't do enlisted men's work."

Without another word, the bystander threw off his cloak. He joined the soldiers and within a few minutes the heavy log was in place.

"I suppose I should thank you," sneered the corporal.

"Not necessary at all," answered the gentleman, putting on his cloak. "I'm happy to have helped. Any time you need an extra hand, just let me know."

"And where can I reach you?" demanded the corporal.

"You will generally find me at headquarters," replied the gentleman. "The name is Washington."

Jesus was this kind of man — always offering the extra hand. By personal example, He made selflessness and service the standard of discipleship. "If any man would come after me, let him deny himself and take up his cross and follow me" (Mark 8:34). The members of His cabinet did just this. With no thought for their own safety, they healed the sick (*see* Acts 3:1–10), defied the authorities (*see* Acts 4:19, 20), and enthusiastically gave themselves to the proclamation of the good news of the gospel. That they furnished us with an enviable record of usefulness and service is evidenced by the fact that no less than six of them died as martyrs for their Lord. Once notoriously undisciplined, disorderly, and disorganized, the disciples became a unified force, singular in their faith, devoted to the task of being servants of all mankind.

If we would become Christian disciples in today's world, we cannot escape the imperative of studying the lives of these men who were members of Jesus' cabinet. Had it not been for them, our image of Jesus might well have perished from human memory.

II

Jesus' Cabinet

and he appointed twelve, to be with him . . .
Simon whom he surnamed Peter;
James the son of Zebedee
and John the brother of James,
whom he surnamed Boanerges, that is, sons of thunder;
Andrew,
and Philip,
and Bartholomew,
and Matthew,
and Thomas,
and James the son of Alphaeus,
and Thaddaeus,
and Simon the Cananaean,
and Judas Iscariot, who betrayed him.

Mark 3:16–19

1

Destroyed by Wrong Choices

History is replete with stories of treachery and deceit. When Julius Caesar was on his way to the Roman forum, he was attacked by his political enemies. Each had promised to thrust his sword deep into Caesar's flesh. Naturally, Caesar reeled and stumbled under the force of that onslaught. The pain suffered from their vicious blows was excruciating. Still, he made no cry. Caesar turned and saw that one of his closest friends was also among the attackers and sobbed, "You, too, Brutus?"

At one time Benedict Arnold was a loyal citizen of the United States, a brave soldier, a gallant five-star general. His name was highly regarded. He even enjoyed the friendship of George Washington. During the Revolutionary War he saw five subordinates promoted over his head, and the blow to his pride was more than he could take. The injury so rankled in his breast that he laid plans to get revenge. He was commissioned a brigadier general in the British army and for twenty thousand dollars in compensation for property losses surrendered the fort at West Point. He moved to Great Britain but was scorned and neglected by the English. He died a most unhappy man.

The most perfidious betrayal ever recorded is the story of Judas Iscariot. By placing the kiss of death on the cheek of his Lord, he immediately set himself apart as the chief of collaborators, the finest of the fifth columnists, the tip-top turncoat, or, as some writers describe him, the devil's most dedicated disciple. Why, then, did Jesus give him the rank of a cabinet member? For the same reason as He did the others. He recognized Judas Iscariot's tremendous potentiality, his innate leadership qualities. He saw that he was capable of becoming an extraordinary person, a dynamic disciple.

Judas was born and reared in Keroith, located about ten miles south of Hebron and thirty miles south of Jerusalem, close to the Sinai desert, the only member of Jesus' cabinet from Judea.

He was given an honorable name. When properly interpreted *Judas* means praise of God. It was a popular appellation among the Jews. In 167 B.C. a man by the name of Judas Maccabaeus led the Israelites in a revolt against their conquerors, the Greeks, and somehow managed to win their independence. Almost immediately he was heralded as a national hero. What George Washington is for Americans, Judas Maccabaeus was to the Jews of the first century. Since *Judas* was a name which represented the very finest in character, Judas Iscariot wore it proudly.

He also had the good fortune of being reared in a God-fearing home. His parents must have cultivated in him an inquiring mind, a tender heart, and a courageous spirit for when Jesus appeared with His lofty ideals and great purposes he was willing to forsake everything to follow Him. No pressure was put on him. He was not forced in any way. Judas Iscariot volunteered for service in Christ's cause. Unlike Matthew and some of the other disciples, he had no mean reputation to overcome. There was no blemish in his life to be erased. From the beginning, Judas was a man of integrity, enthusiastic about the work to which he had tendered his services.

Notice, too, that his fellow cabinet members held him in highest esteem. There was no undercurrent of disrespect. Not one among them ever suspected him of foul play, of stealing from the common purse. Even in the Upper Room on the occasion of the Last Supper when Jesus said, "One of you will betray me" (Matthew 26:21), no disciple pointed an accusing finger at him and said, "Thou Judas, are the man!" Perceiving their own capability of committing the crime, each looked into his own heart and said, "Is it I, Lord?" (Matthew 26:22).

James Smithson cultivated the practice of illustrating the wide margins of his Bible. Opposite the story of Judas Iscariot and his betrayal of Jesus, he drew the picture of a baby lying in a cradle. It had a sweet face and big, wondering eyes. Beneath the picture he wrote the name "Judas Iscariot." It was his way of saying that as a child Judas was innocent, that he was free to grow as he would. This writer is in agreement with Smithson's evaluation. Judas Iscariot was potentially a great Christian leader. Jesus gave him the status of a cabinet member because of what he could contribute to the Kingdom of God, but somewhere along the way he fell from grace. Judas Iscariot misused his talent, prostituted his ability, and disintegrated as a person until, in the epitome of deceit, he betrayed his Lord.

There is a glorious winged creature, a butterfly, potentially hidden away beneath the repulsive exterior of the crawling caterpillar. All caterpillars do not become butterflies. Entomologists tell us a fly sometimes thrusts a tiny egg into the body of the caterpillar. The egg hatches into a grub which feeds upon the butterfly, forming elements in the makeup of that caterpillar. The caterpillar suffers no pain and does not feel that anything is amiss. It goes right on eating and growing and living its life as a worm, but its wings do not appear. The grub has destroyed its capacity to advance. The glorious winged creature which might have been is gone. It can never become a butterfly. Judas Iscariot can be likened to one of these unfortunate caterpillars. He never achieved his true manhood, nor blossomed as a disciple. Somewhere a grub pierced his heart and arrested his growth. Was it foreordination? G. Campbell Morgan, one of this century's great expository preachers, said, "I do not believe that Judas was a man in the ordinary sense of the word. I believe that he was a devil incarnate, created in history for the nefarious work that was hell's work." His explanation raises more questions than it settles. If Judas was created a devil incarnate and sent into the world to fulfill ancient prophecies, then he was no more to blame for what he did than the vessel that is spoiled by the potter. Under these circumstances, God would have been responsible. This view we cannot accept. Traitors and scoundrels are made, not born.

Was the grub impatience? No doubt Judas shared the expectation of the disciples that Jesus' Kingdom would be an earthly dominion. He must have frequently posed the query: Why the delay? Why did Jesus not exercise His authority? If the betrayal was his way of forcing the Master to begin a revolution that would usher in the Kingdom of God, perhaps impatience was the grub that destroyed his life. However, this is a most charitable explanation.

Was the grub greed? The Scriptures do say, "For the love of money is the root of all evils" (1 Timothy 6:10), and the price of betrayal was thirty pieces of silver. But the amount of money gained, equivalent to only twenty-one dollars or the price of a slave, was hardly enough to tempt a man to betray One he loved. The reward was pitifully little for so sinister a deed. Furthermore, why did he return the money? Explain the sudden feeling of remorse. The coins in his purse should have been comfort enough had Judas's sole motivation been avarice.

Was the grub vindictiveness? Judas may have betrayed Jesus to get revenge for the rebuke given when Mary anointed the feet of the Master with costly ointment (*see* John 12:1–11). But he was a sensible, calculating, and intelligent man so he must have known that vengeance is never sweet.

What, then, was the grub that destroyed his life? It was a series of wrong choices. Judas was the victim of a smoldering resentment. Being the only disciple from Judea, he often felt the aloneness of being an outsider. His language, customs, and traditions set him apart from the others. He was not a Galilean, and the sense of estrangement is fertile soil for antisocial behavior.

Then there were cliques among the Twelve. All did not share equally in the Master's confidence. Peter, James, and John especially formed an inner circle of friendship in which Judas, perhaps the brightest and best trained of the group, was not included. It disappointed him, and exclusiveness is an environment in which jealousy flourishes.

Perhaps he felt Jesus was a poor business associate. As manager of the purse, Judas felt a keen sense of responsibility for the developing of itineraries and the systematic payment of accounts. But Jesus, though practical and realistic in matters of faith and morals, disregarded such things. He sent the disciples on crusades without money or script (*see* Luke 10:4) and taught them to have no thought for tomorrow (*see* Matthew 6:34). This unbusinesslike approach perturbed Judas.

Furthermore, he was dissatisfied. Judas had envisioned an earthly kingdom, where he would share in the glory of government. But Jesus' message was otherworldly. He talked more about spiritual than temporal matters. He even encouraged His followers to love their enemies. These ideas, too impractical to initiate a revolution, abetted Judas's disappointment and animosity.

Some say he was a double-minded man, torn between love of the Master and love of money, between a sincere desire to see the Kingdom of God come and selfish ambition. Since much conduct is the result of inner conflicts that never rise to the level of conscious thought, this may be a perceptive analysis.

Judas stole from the common purse. He did not intend to, but, so many forces were at war within him, it was an escape. At first, he rationalized by saying he would replace the money, that what he took was part payment for his legitimate salary. Besides, the amount pilfered was trifling in proportion to what he could have made had he not given up his business to set out on this mad adventure. Judas may have duped himself into believing he was not stealing. He may have kept his thievery from the disciples, but there was One he did not deceive, who knew him for what he was. The disappointment and grief which he saw reflected in Jesus' kindly eyes exposed his secret. He began to feel miserable and uncomfortable in the presence of the Master. His deep-seated guilt prompted him to put the blame for the change, not on himself, but on Jesus. Judas came to hate this onetime Friend with a bitter hatred.

When called to be an apostle, Judas had possibilities of becoming a great Christian leader, but he developed in the opposite direction. He was a long while bringing himself to the place where he was willing to betray his Lord, but the grub of wrong choices bolstered by a smoldering resentment eventually succeeded in destroying his life. When he deposited the kiss of death on Jesus' cheek, it was like the last drop of water that causes a glass to overflow. It terminated his association with the Twelve, signaled the final corruption of his character, and forever set apart the name, *Judas,* as a symbol of vileness and deceit.

Now we ask the final question: Does the story of his infamy project a message for life today? Yes, in three ways. First, Judas epitomizes sin. He describes it as pleasant only in anticipation. Young people in love sometimes feel strongly the desire to go all the way in expressing that love. At the time, their happiness seems to depend upon that ultimate expression. However, once the act has been consummated, its beauty is forever lost. Guilt and shame are awakened within the conscience. Sex out of wedlock is always attractive only in anticipation.

Businessmen occasionally devise questionable schemes to further their work. At the time, it is as if their whole future hinges upon the success of some such transaction. However, once the scheme has been perfected and the transaction completed, the pleasure disappears. In its place comes sorrow and regret.

Judas looked forward to the betrayal. Maybe he thought it would force the hand of Jesus; maybe it was an attempt at revenge; maybe it was a final manifestation of greed. But whatever pleasure he derived from the deed, it came only in anticipation. Once the kiss had been placed on the cheek of the Master, Judas felt contempt and remorse. The feeling was so intense he tried to get rid of it by giving up his coins. When this failed, he fled out into the night, grabbed up a piece of rope and hanged himself.

Judas depicts sin as habitual. One day, when the sun was hot, a young man walked along a dusty road and looked in vain for a shady spot in which to rest. Suddenly he saw a towering rock nearby and found at its base the opening of a cave. He was just about to enter when he noticed a beautiful woman sitting at a spinning wheel.

"Madam," said the man, "I am weary and worn. May I rest in this cool shade?"

"Surely you may," said the woman, "if you will but let me wind about you some of this silken thread. 'Tis all I ask — just a whim of mine."

"Indeed, madam," said the man, "wind your thread about me as I lie and when I am rested I will snap it asunder and go my way."

The young man lay down in the cool shade, and as he watched her quick fingers wind the thread about him and listened to the song she sang, he went to sleep. At length he awoke and started to rise, but was amazed to find he could not move hand or foot. He found that the thread that was wound around him in thousands of coils was no longer bright like silk, but dull and drab and each coil was the size of a rope. His companion was no longer a beautiful woman but a witch, who laughed at his vain endeavor to free himself.

Something similar happened to Judas. He did not mean to go wrong. He did not become a disciple with the intention of committing history's most dastardly crime. At first he was just disappointed and jealous. Then he began to borrow funds from the common purse. He meant to pay it back but never got around to it. Then his selfishness demanded more. One thing led to another until at last he was caught in an unbreakable web of sin. He relived the legend of the silk thread. Habitual sin turned Judas Iscariot, once an honored apostle, into a traitor.

Judas says, in addition, that sin produces frightening consequences. It is like a canoeist taking the wrong passage through a white water shoal. Upon entering the shoal he is free to choose his passage. Once in the fast water he has no alternative but to submit to the current. If the choice be bad the outcome will probably be tragic. Boiling white water is a power over which the canoeist has little control.

Judas was free to betray or not to betray Jesus, but once the course was set he was not free from the guilt and shame which followed. In the words of John A. Redhead, "Right is right and wrong is wrong, it is never right to do wrong and we can't do wrong and feel right about it." The penalty for trespassing against the laws of God can be severe.

Judas describes sin. He also provides insight into the nature of man. He suggests that a good start is not enough. Like the rash builder in Jesus' parable, Judas set out to build a tower. He made an impressive beginning. He was reared in a good home; he was given an honorable name; he volunteered for service in Christ's cause. But he was not able to complete the tower. A good life — like a sterling performance in athletics — if it is to count in eternity's final reckoning, must be coupled with a good ending.

Judas advances the idea that a man can be close to Christ and still fall away. W. E. Sangster tells of a brilliant young lawyer who was climbing the mountain near Abner Falls in North Wales with a friend. His friend noticed the green slime on the rocks as they climbed and called out: "Do be careful," to which the young Mr. Payne replied: "Oh, it's as safe as anything. I couldn't fall here." They were the last words he uttered. His mangled body was picked up at the bottom of the falls.

Judas was one of the Twelve, a member of Jesus' cabinet, a personal friend of our Lord. He lived with Him, taught with Him, witnessed His miracles, became a dedicated disciple. Yet, somehow, he fell away. It is possible to be in Christ's company, a member of His church, and be guilty of the foulest betrayal. An excessive amount of self-confidence can be dangerous.

Judas describes sin. He provides insight into the nature of man. He also advances something vital about the character of God. He intimates that God provides man with every opportunity to be redeemed, that His forgiveness is limitless. Jesus did all He could to save Judas for the church. He included him among His special circle of friends, entrusted him with the treasury, honored him with the first sop at the Last Supper, and, in the Garden of Gethsemane, with his traitorous kiss still hot upon His cheek, called him, "Friend." Jesus saw Judas at his worst yet spoke to him tenderly. There was no condemnation, only love. It was a final gesture of entreaty. He would have forgiven His betrayer. Judas failed to grasp his opportunity and so died the most tragic figure in history.

2

The Dreamer

One of the special days in the Christian calendar year—though of minor importance so far as most people are concerned—is August 24, or Saint Bartholomew's Day. The occasion marks the anniversary of the "Massacre of St. Bartholomew," a tragic event that took place in Paris in 1572 when 30,000 Huguenots fighting for religious liberty met their death. The massacre bears the name *Bartholomew* because of the realistic way medieval artists had portrayed his martyrdom. He was bound securely, flayed with knives, and then crucified. (The knives that were used to kill Bartholomew were similar to those used today for skinning animals. They are the symbol most frequently used to represent this disciple.) It was a brutal death. Knowing this, we can understand how the Huguenots came to associate the stark and the terrible with his name. Certainly what happened that day in Paris during the religious wars of the sixteenth century was barbaric.

Bartholomew is mentioned as a member of Jesus' cabinet in all three of the Synoptic Gospels and in the Book of Acts

33

(*see* Matthew 10:3; Mark 3:18; Luke 6:14; Acts 1:13). Aside from these four references, the New Testament tells nothing about him—that is, unless we can assume he and Nathanael are the same person. The matter has been a subject of considerable controversy and religious leaders are still debating the issue. Generally it is conceded that Bartholomew and Nathanael are the same disciple. William Barclay, one of the most authoritative of the contemporary Bible scholars, is very definitely of this opinion. He gives three reasons for it. First, Bartholomew is not itself a first name. It is a distinguishing second name like Smith or Jones. It identified him with his father. Since *Bar* means son of, *Bartholomew* probably means son of Tholmai. This being the case, there is nothing to deter us from believing Nathanael is simply Bartholomew's first name.

Secondly, they are closely related in the biblical text. While the fourth gospel does not mention Bartholomew, it does tell about Nathanael. John gives him such a prominent place in the text that one is led to believe (even though it is never clearly stated) that he was a disciple. If Nathanael was one of the Twelve (and there is no valid reason to doubt it), we have no alternative but to accept the fact that the Bartholomew of the Synoptics and the Nathanael of John are the same person.

Thirdly, there was a mutual friendship. In the listing of the disciples in the first three gospels, the names of Philip and Bartholomew always occur together and in the fourth gospel it is Philip who brought Nathanael to Jesus. Therefore, since Philip is associated with both Bartholomew and Nathanael in the biblical narrative, we can reasonably assume that Bartholomew and Nathanael are one and the same person.

Proof of this identity falls short of certainty. I should be the first to admit this. But for purposes of our discussion, we shall be using the names interchangeably as though they were in fact one person.

Look first at Bartholomew prior to his conversion. His home was the little village of Cana in Galilee (*see* John 21:2), three and one-half or four miles northeast of Nazareth, a rival community. He enjoyed stretching out in the shade, away from the heat and the hurry of the day, to read from the Scriptures and to pray. A fig tree situated at the front door of his house provided him just such a place of retreat. Nathanael is pictured as reclining under it the first time he appears in the text of the fourth gospel (*see* John 1:48). The scene gives some insight into his character and personality. For one thing, he knew how to live with silence. Here is a discipline more frequently praised than practiced. When not talking, we are being talked to by the radio, television, record player, or some other talking machine. One or more of these devices can probably be found in every room of the modern home, in most places of public assembly, and in our private and public vehicles of transportation. On those rare occasions when we are alone with our thoughts, we sometimes find the solitude so frustrating we have to turn on one of these devices in order to maintain our sanity. Yet, Arnold J. Toynbee in his book *A Study of History,* an exhaustive study of the rise of civilizations, believes that the creative personalities who founded the great civilizations drew their power from the Nathanael-like quality of withdrawal and meditation. He says:

> Creative personalities, when they are taking the mystic path which is their highest level . . . pass first out of action into ecstasy. . . . The withdrawal makes it possible for the personality to realize powers within himself which might have remained dormant if he had not been released for the time being from his social toils and trammels. Such a withdrawal may be a voluntary action on his part or it may be forced upon him by circumstances beyond his control; in either case the withdrawal is an opportunity,

and perhaps a necessary condition, for the anchorite's transfiguration; "anchorite," in the original Greek, means literally "one who goes apart."

Then Toynbee illustrates this thesis by reference to Moses on the mountain, Plato in the cave, Jesus in the wilderness, Paul's three years in Arabia, Gregory's long period of self-withdrawal, and other like examples.

Nathanael knew how to live with silence, but he also had a great capacity for dreams. No telling how many times, under that same fig tree, he and his friend Philip envisioned the coming of the Messiah and the restoration of Israel to its proper place among the kingdoms of the world! The student of John's Gospel feels they must have had at least conversations about these great issues.

Dr. J. Kenneth Shamblin tells of a couple who moved to this country. They did not understand our language very well, but they had risked all the money they had on a lottery and had won six thousand dollars. When they were paid, they took the six thousand dollars to their bank with great happiness in their hearts. Then, after much confusion because they could not understand the language well, they were made to understand that they had been paid off in counterfeit money. The police were called; the husband panicked and tried to escape because he was afraid they would think he was involved in the counterfeiting crime. The wife finally tricked her husband into giving himself up. He discovered that instead of wanting him as an accomplice to the crime, the police simply needed him to be a witness against the people who had been carrying on this crooked scheme. The story ended with the couple walking into their shabby apartment returning to the dull routine of daily duty. The man took his wife's hand in his and said, "Now we must go back to our ten-cent dreams."

Many times it has been the same with us. We, too, have had our ten-cent dreams. We have been satisfied to give our minds, our time, and our lives to those things which are small and insignificant. But not Nathanael! He looked forward to the coming of the King of Israel. He longed to be a better man, was always aspiring, resolving, and praying. There in the garden of his own home, he found a place where he could be alone with his thoughts and dream great dreams. Oh, how he must have longed for their fulfillment!

What happened to Bartholomew? He did not long remain this quiet, reserved, and contemplative person. Jesus came into his life and his character was transformed, his personality revolutionized. He was converted as quickly as he met the Master. Bartholomew came from beneath the fig tree, left its shade and security to become involved with Him in the heartache and suffering of humanity. No longer content just to meditate and pray, he became a soldier of the cross, a man of action.

There is considerable speculation that Nathanael was present at the wedding feast in Cana of Galilee, that he was one of the disciples on the road to Emmaus. As a close traveling companion of Jesus, he must have been witness to many of the healing miracles and sensed the deepening loyalty and devotion of the Twelve. Surely he observed their widening sphere of influence for everything Jesus touched was changed, enobled, and glorified. John says that after the Crucifixion Nathanael was a member of the party of seven former disciples who signed on a boat at Capernaum. Led by Peter, they fished all night but caught nothing. Morning found them so tired, disgusted, and discouraged they headed their boat toward shore. In the faint light of the new day, one of them suddenly noticed a Man standing on the beach. Presently they were able to make out His features. It was none other than Jesus.

When they beached the boat, a hearty breakfast which He had prepared was ready and waiting (*see* John 21:1–14). The seven disciples, one of whom was Nathanael, were overcome by the realization that their Spiritual Leader was not dead, that God had not withdrawn His love. They renewed their vows and went on to become pillars in the founding of the Christian Church.

Tradition says Nathanael traveled extensively, giving himself for others, spending himself in selfless service. In the end, he suffered a terrible and brutal death that the name of Jesus Christ might be glorified.

How did it happen? What brought about this transformation of character and personality? For one thing, it was the power of a personal friendship. When Nathanael's meditation was broken by Philip's breathless announcement, "We have found him of whom Moses in the law and also the prophets wrote, Jesus of Nazareth, the son of Joseph" (John 1:45), he hesitated to believe. "Can anything good come out of Nazareth?" (John 1:46). After all, Nazareth was a town of no mean reputation. It was so small and insignificant. Surely the Messiah would first appear in Jerusalem! But somehow that friendly conversation enabled Nathanael to overcome this prejudice. When Philip said, "Come and see" (John 1:46), he went.

Secondly, there was the towering personality of Jesus. When Jesus saw Philip bringing Nathanael to Him, He said, "Behold, an Israelite indeed, in whom is no guile!" (John 1:47). The world saw Nathanael as an idle dreamer, a cynic, but Jesus saw him as something infinitely more—as a man of intelligence, conviction, sincerity, and depth. He saw him as a dynamic disciple. So His first words to Nathanael were words of approval, commendation, and praise.

The scene demonstrates the power of a positive appeal. Nathanael asked, "How do you know me?" Jesus answered, "Before Philip called you, when you were under the fig tree, I saw you" (John 1:48). Such was the persuasive power of the Master.

The third major influence upon the life of His young and energetic disciple was the force of a faultless faith. Here was a Man who had looked into Nathanael's heart, who had touched the spring of his soul, who had seen him at his best, who knew him as he had never been known before, who had spoken to the holiest in him. There was something about Him so attractive, so irresistible Nathanael could not hold back. "Rabbi," he said, "you are the Son of God! You are the King of Israel!" (John 1:49). It was not a rational decision but the work of faith. He could not describe why he had made this commitment, but it was an unconditional surrender. Unlike Julius Caesar, who said, "I came, I saw, I conquered," Nathanael came, saw, and was overcome. The miracle of belief had, in the twinkling of an eye, led him from prejudice to purity, from cynicism to certitude, from dreamer to disciple.

William P. Barker tells in his book, *Twelve Who Were Chosen*, about someone who was going on at length about Christianity being of questionable substance. "A very wise friend quietly pointed up to some stained glass windows of a church building. From the outside the windows seemed grimy and grey-colored.

" 'Don't look like much, do they, from out here?' he said. The critic agreed.

" 'Now come with me.' The wise friend led the way inside the church, and there, on the inside, the light was shining through the windows, bringing out all the gorgeous colors and rich patterns of a figure of Christ.

"You have to be on the inside to see Him. If you stand on the outside and discuss and argue with Him forever, He will mean little to you.

"Get on the inside, into the fellowship of the church, if you are not an active member already.

"Get on the inside, into the pages of the Bible, if you have not done so.

"Get on the inside, into His presence, by getting on your knees and turning yourself over to Him, admitting you need His help and humbly asking for it.

"Get on the inside, into an attitude of taking Him seriously.

"Then you will see Him more than just another man. You will find He is the Teacher, the Son of God and the King! Nathanael did!"

He got on the inside, became a member of Jesus' cabinet, and it made a decided difference in the quality of his life. It always does.

3

The Obscure Disciple

Three men named James are mentioned in the New Testament. There is James, the son of Zebedee, a brother of the beloved disciple John and one of the Sons of Thunder. There is James, the brother of our Lord. He was not a disciple, but later emerged as one of the established leaders in the Jerusalem segment of the church. There is James, the son of Alphaeus, who will be the subject of discussion in this chapter. He is the most obscure of all the members of Jesus' cabinet. Nowhere in the Scriptures is mentioned anything that he said or did. Only his name is recorded. However, it is significant that his name appears in every list of the Twelve including the roll call of those who, after the death and Resurrection of Jesus, formed the nucleus of the earliest Christian church. One other clue to his character is found in the Gospel of Mark. A woman at the scene of the Crucifixion is called Mary the mother of James the Less, or the Minor, or the Younger, depending on the translation you read. Otherwise, this young and dynamic disciple remains a forgotten man. What, then, can be said in his behalf?

For one thing, he was a short man. This can be inferred by taking liberties with the nickname, James the Less, or as some translators prefer, James the Little, a nickname which was probably given to him by Jesus. When we speak of Little George or Little John, referring to a child, the name is given a tender and affectionate flavor. But let the child become a man and call him Little and the flavor of the title changes. There is a hint of contempt ranging from kindly indifference to rudeness, causing the small-statured person considerable mental anguish. This attitude generally becomes apparent when the undersized person is in the society of the young, the brutish, or the ignorant. In biblical times, little men were continually made aware of their shortcomings. The Jews were proudly intolerant of little people. The deformed and the retarded were ridiculed and often kept in the royal houses as instruments of rough and cruel sport. The Romans frequently measured a man's worth in terms of his inches. They regarded every human body as a possible instrument of war. A man to be worthy of the name had to be ready to engage the enemy at close range and in the ranks of battle every inch counted.

Then Jesus came with an entirely different concept. He denied any correlation between a man's size and his ability to perform. Zacchaeus being a case in point. He judged men not on the basis of their height but on the basis of their hearts; not in terms of their inches but in terms of their inner spirit. Character, He felt, was the only valid gauge of a man's worth. Jesus dealt with James, the son of Alphaeus, on this basis. No doubt, James did not appreciate being called The Less, but the nickname stuck and we continue to remember him by it. James may have been of small stature physically, but we have good reason to believe he was a big man otherwise. Jesus chose him to be a member of His cabinet.

He was reared in a God-fearing home. Describing the

scene of the Crucifixion, Mark says: "There were also women looking on from afar, among whom were Mary Magdalene and Mary the mother of James the younger" (Mark 15:40). The presence of his mother at the cross indicates a love for Jesus Christ which places her in the inner circle of women who followed Him. She must have been a deeply religious person and her home a place where God was real and His presence known.

Rufus Jones, the great Quaker philosopher, had the good fortune of growing up in such an atmosphere of faith. He once wrote in his book *Finding the Trail of Life,* "While I was too young to have any religion of my own, I had come to a home where religion kept its fires always burning. We had very few 'things,' but were rich in invisible wealth. I was not 'christened' in a church, but I was sprinkled from morning until night with the dew of religion. We never ate a meal which did not begin with a hush of thanksgiving, we never began a day without a 'family gathering' at which mother read a chapter of the Bible, after which there would follow a weighty silence. These silences, during which all the children of the family were hushed with a kind of awe, were very important features of my spiritual development. There was work inside and outside the house waiting to be done, and yet we sat there hushed and quiet, doing nothing. I very quickly discovered that something real was taking place. We were feeling our way down to that place from which living words come, and very often they did come. Someone would bow and talk to God so simple and quietly that he never seemed far away. . . . My first steps in religion were thus acted. It was a religion which we did together."

Such was the legacy of James, the son of Alphaeus. He was prepared for discipleship by living in a God-fearing home. His parents were very likely disappointed when Matthew, assumed by some to be their son, drifted into the field of tax collecting. Their hearts may have been broken a second time when James followed suit. But the ancient proverb, "Train up a child in the way he should go, and when he is old he will not depart from it" (Proverbs 22:6), came to life in these two boys. The religious disciplines taught within the family coupled with the example of consecrated parents eventually bore fruit. Both Matthew and James became members of Jesus' cabinet.

Finally, this dynamic disciple is the patron saint of all those quiet, unassuming, little people whose unheralded and unknown contributions have been the backbone of progress. If James, the son of Alphaeus, rendered any service—and I am confident that he rendered a great deal because his name appears in the list of the Twelve after the death and Resurrection of Jesus and because tradition, however unreliable, says he preached in Persia and that he suffered a martyr's death—it went unrecognized. Everything he said and did passed unnoticed.

Eleven-year-old Austin Gollaher was swimming with an eight-year-old friend who was seized with cramps and was drowning. Risking his own life, this young man brought his comrade to shore. No one knows Austin Gollaher, but the world will never forget the man whom he saved. His name is Abraham Lincoln.

In the city of Boston there once lived a man by the name of Kimball. He was an humble shoe-store manager. Very few have heard of him. Yet it was he who introduced Dwight L. Moody, the great evangelist, to Jesus Christ.

James, the son of Alphaeus, belongs in this company. The Scriptures may be silent about his role in the development of the church, but in his own modest way he made a significant contribution. He just did not mind who got the credit.

The obituary of an actor read, "Though never a star, he was invaluable in small parts."

I sing the song of unknown men, of names you rarely hear
Whose actions fired and words inspired the heroes we
  hold dear.

I sing the song of unknown men, strong men of faith and
  power,
By word and deed they sowed the seed, their blessing
  grows each hour.

I sing the song of unknown men, time does not dim their
  glow,
No thrill of fame or crowds acclaim was their mid-life's
  deep woe.

I sing the song of unknown men who never know life's
  praise.
Because they cared and greatly dared, they lived to bless
  our days.

I sing the song of unknown men who prove that love is
  might,
No more alone, no more unknown, they live in heaven's
  light.

                                        JOHN L. STICKLEY

James, the son of Alphaeus, was a charter member of this grand and glorious group. He was unknown and unremembered yet rendered a vital ministry to the church.

4

A Son of Thunder

The Security Council of the United Nations has been domi-
nated by four major world powers: The United States, Great
Britain, France, and Soviet Russia. To these nations has been
given the right of veto, a privilege which on many occasions
has been a stumbling block in the path of progress. Nevertheless, these major world powers are today recognized as the
Big Four in international relations.

Compare the cabinet of Jesus Christ with the United
Nations Security Council and you will discover that it, too,
had an intimate inner circle. The members of this executive
committee were Peter, James, and John. Granted they did not
have the right of veto, but Jesus did take them into His
confidence. He granted them privileges the other disciples
did not enjoy.

They alone among the Twelve were present at the raising
of Jairus' daughter (*see* Luke 8:49–51); accompanied Him on
the trek up the Mount of Transfiguration (*see* Matthew 17:1, 2);
witnessed His agony in the Garden of Gethsemane (*see*
Mark 14:32, 33). This intimate association gave their state-
ments authority. Men listened whenever one of them voiced
an opinion. They were Jesus' chief spokesmen. No wonder

historians speak of Peter, James, and John as the Big Three among the apostolic band.

In this chapter, we are to focus our attention upon the second member of this elite fellowship. James, the son of Zebedee, was born and reared along the shores of beautiful Lake Galilee. As a boy, he swam and played in its clear blue waters. As a man, he joined his father Zebedee, his brother John, and their partners, Andrew and Simon, in the fishing business. Today that business might be listed as Zebedee and Sons, Inc., because they operated a whole fleet of fishing boats and had hired servants. Generally they sold their fish in their hometown of Bethsaida, or in Capernaum. Occasionally when their catch was large, they would salt down some of the fish and ship them to Jerusalem and other inland cities.

It is reasonable to assume that James was successful in business, that he was respected in the community, and congenial in his personal relationships. He was not just an ordinary fellow. He was well above the average in talent and ability. You might say he was an extraordinary person. Perhaps this is why Jesus selected him to be a member of His cabinet.

Three words are descriptive of James's spiritual journey. The first is *decision*. He and his brother John were mending their nets when Jesus approached, looked them full in the face, and called them to become fishers of men (*see* Matthew 4:21, 22). Like the Israelites who were suddenly confronted with Moses' leadership and a possible exodus while suffering the humiliation of slavery in Egypt, these two men stood at a major crossroad. They could either remain at home and enjoy the relative security of their business or leave home and follow Jesus with all the dangers and deprivations His way of life offered. On the one hand, there was bondage with bread; on the other, freedom with uncertainty. Remembering how the Israelites turned their eyes toward the wilderness and beheld the glory of the Lord, James and John looked into the face of Jesus and saw the Messiah. Then, like their forebears, they took the dare, forsook everything, and followed Him whom they felt was the Son of God.

It appears to have been an impromptu decision. Actually, it was preceded by a long period of preparation. For years James and his brother had been restless and dissatisfied. They were tired of Roman domination and longed for Israel to be self-governed. Moreover, their religious life lacked a certain spiritual quality that affluence had not been able to satisfy. Perhaps this is the reason they were attracted to John the Baptist. His message stirred within their breasts a new hope. The sons of Zebedee were so moved by what he said that they answered his call to repentance and were baptized in the River Jordan.

Then Jesus came. John the Baptist pointed Him out as the One who would fulfill the ancient prophecy as the long-awaited Messiah of the Jews. No doubt these brothers talked at length about this Man from Nazareth and about His mission. Their friend Andrew, along with an unnamed companion, had heard Him speak and had been convinced that He was the Son of God. No wonder James and John were open and receptive to Jesus' call. Their interest had already been aroused. It was a gradual awakening, but when the opportunity came, they committed themselves to a loyalty higher than anything they had ever known. They said in essence, "Here am I [Lord]! Send me" (Isaiah 6:8).

Zebedee did not appreciate this decision. He knew he would be forced to sell his business if the boys left home. He could not carry on alone, but James and John were determined. They sincerely believed Jesus offered a way of life that would bring the contentment for which they yearned. Without hesitation they dropped their nets, packed up their personal belongings, and left everything—even their disappointed father—to become His disciples.

The second word that describes James's spiritual journey is *transformation*. Upon accepting Jesus' call, James effected some revolutionary changes in his life. By nature James was an intense person, hotheaded and violent. His quick temper showed itself on at least one occasion (*see* Luke 9:51–55). Enroute to Jerusalem the apostolic party stopped at a Samaritan village in the hope of finding lodging for the night. But the Samaritans, because of their hatred and prejudice against the Jews, refused them this hospitality. When word of the denial reached James, he went up in smoke. His face turned white hot with anger. He said to Jesus, "Would You like for us to command fire to come down from heaven and destroy this unworthy village? Who do they think they are—these half-breeds, these Samaritans—to deny the Messiah entrance?" Jesus replied, "James, you do not understand the spirit that wells up within you. The Son of Man did not come to destroy men's lives, but to save them." Then, to further illustrate the commandment, "You shall love the Lord your God . . . with all your soul . . . and your neighbor as yourself" (Luke 10:27), He told the beautiful story of the Good Samaritan.

This experience led James to see how contrary to the will of God is the spirit of vengeance and violence. It made him realize his own quick temper was self-centered and dangerous. He learned, as did the ancient prophet Elijah, that the fire from heaven and the sword of human hate will never bring in God's Kingdom. Only the power of love or an outgoing good-will is adequate to change men's ways. It took him a long while, but under the influence of Jesus, James's violent nature was transformed. He became an effective and creative instrument in the building of the church.

James was also ambitious. He wanted to be at the head of the class, the big shot or the top banana. No wonder his feelings were hurt when he overheard Jesus say to Simon, who he felt was a man of lesser ability, "You are Peter, and on this rock I will build my church" (Matthew 16:18). He did not like the thought of being relegated to a lesser position. The more he brooded over the matter, the worse it got. Envy and jealousy began to take root in his heart. Then James discovered that his brother, John, felt the same way. Together they talked about the situation with their mother, who by this time had also become one of Jesus' followers. She had even furthered His cause by giving Him most of the proceeds from the sale of her late husband's estate. She loved Jesus a great deal, but, at this point, she loved her children more. The thought of His not taking full advantage of their natural abilities upset her. She then joined James and John in fanning the flames of ambition. Together they began to plot how to keep Peter from being first on Jesus' staff (*see* Mark 10:35–39). They even made the bold request, "Teacher, we want You to do for us whatever we ask of You."

Jesus replied, "What do you want Me to do for you?"

They said, "Grant us to sit, one at Your right hand and the other on Your left, in Your glory."

Did you ever witness such egotism? The very idea of asking for special consideration! Yet Jesus kept His poise. "You do not know what you are asking," He said. "Are you able to drink the cup that I drink, or to be baptized with the baptism with which I am baptized?"

They answered, "We are able."

It was a long time before James proved that he was able. There was the patient leadership of Jesus and the support of his fellow disciples; there was the Upper Room experience and the lesson in humility; there was the ordeal of the cross and the ensuing loneliness and grief; there was the Easter victory and the hope it brought into full view. Jesus had said, ". . . whoever would be great among you must be your servant, and whoever would be first among you must be your slave; even as the Son of man came not to be served but to serve, and to give his life as a ransom for many" (Matthew 20:26-28). James did not grasp the full significance of these words until after the Resurrection. Then the Pentecost came. Heavenly fire fell on the disciples. It burned not with flames of destruction but with the pure and holy flame of love for all mankind. The experience worked the final transformation. James no longer sulked because Jesus would not guarantee him first place. He was perfectly willing to take a backseat and let Peter become the acknowledged leader of the church. His new desire was to tender only a self-effacing service for Jesus Christ.

Arthur H. Madsen wanted to be a missionary, but his age was against him. One day he approached his wife with the idea of becoming a carpenter for Christ. Receiving her consent, he left his regular construction work and began an unusual ministry of building for the Lord without accepting fixed wages. That was eighteen years ago. Today hundreds of churches of different denominations, Christian schools, and Bible camps have benefited from his skill. A friend once asked him, "Couldn't you lead a good Christian life without leaving a steady job for the uncertainties of nomadic work?"

Art answered, "Giving your heart to God is not enough. I believe there has to be a complete change in your life."

This is what happened to James, the son of Zebedee. He met a Man from Nazareth by the name of Jesus and his whole life was changed. His quick temper and selfish ambitions were transformed in such a stellar fashion as to make him a living example of the biblical promise, "If any one is in Christ, he is a new creation; the old has passed away, behold, the new has come" (2 Corinthians 5:17). The transformation gave him freedom, joy, and immeasurable satisfaction.

The third and final word that describes the spiritual journey of this young and dynamic disciple is *service*. Tradition says James left Jerusalem and traveled to Spain where he was the first to preach the gospel to the warmhearted Iberians. There is some question as to the validity of this tradition. Scholars find it hard to believe he could have traveled to such a remote region, done so much creative work, and returned to Jerusalem to die in A.D. 42. Yet remarkably, during the Middle Ages when the Mohammedans were almost taking over in Spain, the influence of his name and the discovery in Ira Flavia of his bones were sufficient to produce a new awakening among the Christians of the ninth century. Today he is called the patron saint of Spain and his bones are said to rest in the celebrated shrine, *Santiago de Compestela,* which means, Saint James of the Field of Stars.

King Herod considered Christianity an heretical movement and resolved to help the Jews stamp it out. Acts says, "About that time Herod the king laid violent hands upon some who belonged to the church. He killed James the brother of John with the sword" (Acts 12:2). Chances are the report would not have been made had James not been a powerful and influential figure. He was the first of the disciples to be martyred.

Eusebius, the early historian, relates an experience that took place at the trial. In James's last hour, the peace and love evident in his face and in his words convicted his accuser. Deeply moved, Josias fell down before him as he was being led away for execution and begged forgiveness, declaring his acceptance of the Christian faith. James lifted Josias to his feet, placed on his forehead the kiss of absolution, and said, "Peace be with you."

Whether or not these records are true, it is evident James did not shrink from the trials of discipleship. A Son of Thunder, his eloquent and persistent witness was invaluable in the development of the church. His life story demonstrates the truth: selfless service is the doorway to the joyful and abundant life.

5

The Beloved Disciple

If I could have one wish for the youth of today, it would be that they cultivate a friendship with the young and dynamic disciple — John, the son of Zebedee. I say this because one good example of the Christian life is worth more than a thousand sermons; one man doing the Christian thing is of more value than a score of men debating the issue. I should like for each young person to have as his hero someone who has excelled in the practice of Christianity.

Football players aspiring to stardom concentrate on the skills and techniques of the finest athletes the game has produced. Would-be poets saturate their minds with the writings of men whose names have outlived the centuries. Potential artists make systematic studies of the master painters. Novice musicians memorize the accomplishments of famous composers. The development of a mature Christian life is no different, nor any easier. To gain mastery here we must study the masters, have as our models those who have known the joys and satisfactions, who have experienced the beauty and grandeur of a life wholly consecrated to God.

John is worthy of just such a place in the hearts of young

men and women. There is something about him that appeals to the intellect, captures the imagination, enlists the emotions, and satisfies one's thirst for action. He represents the best in man. Some adolescents (I say *some* deliberately because most of this generation's youth are of the highest caliber) do not want any help. They think they can be their own teachers, their own inspiration, that they can find their way by their own initiative. Those who travel this road do so at great risk. No man walks alone. To think so is a mistake. Consciously or unconsciously young people will imitate someone. I should wish this someone to be John.

He was the youngest member of Jesus' cabinet. His home was in or about the city of Capernaum. He had a brother James, who, together with Simon Peter, formed an inner circle with their Master. His father operated a fleet of fishing boats on the Sea of Galilee. Their business must have been substantial for there were servants in the home. His mother was Salome. There is a possibility that she was the sister of Mary, the mother of Jesus. If this is true, John and his Lord had ties closer than friendship—they were first cousins.

Tradition says John was a mystic—quiet, reserved, timid, gentle, almost effeminate. Artists have pictured him as a saint with a halo about his head, with hands and face as fine and soft as those of a beautiful woman. But the real John—that is, the John of Synoptic Gospels—was a different kind of man altogether. He was a fisherman, deeply tanned, with skin toughened by constant exposure to the sea breeze, rugged, and sturdy, occasionally given to strong outbursts of feeling. He was as human as one's next-door neighbor. Because he and his brother James were sometimes a whirlwind of enthusiasm and sometimes a tornado of wrath, Jesus nicknamed them Sons of Thunder.

Under the tutelage of his Lord, John became the gallant and wonderful Apostle of Love, the Beloved Disciple.

He is a worthy person for young people to emulate because he learned that tolerance and respect for others is more to be desired than bigotry and self-righteousness. One day he stood on the edge of a crowd surrounding a man possessed of demons. Someone was saying, "In the name of Jesus of Nazareth, come out from him." Hearing the name of his Lord, John naturally pressed closer. As the crowd dispersed, he asked the man doing the healing if he was one of Jesus' disciples. When the man said, "No," he loosed upon him a storm of invectives and commanded him to stop.

Obviously pleased with himself, John reported to Jesus what he had done. "Teacher, we saw a man casting out demons in your name, and we forbade him, because he was not following us" (Mark 9:38). But instead of receiving the approval and commendation of his Lord, John was soundly rebuked. Jesus said, "Do not forbid him. . . . For he that is not against us is for us" (Mark 9:39, 40).

John was so blindly attached to his own particular group he could not see any good in the work of those who belonged to a variant group. He was like the narrow-minded minister who had been helping another clergyman of a different faith with a community project. When the job was done, the second said to the first, "After all, our differences are much less important than our agreements. We are both working for the same great end."

"Yes," replied the other, "we are both doing the Lord's work—you in your way and I in His."

John was so intensely devoted to his own religious persuasion and to the work of the Twelve that he was unaware of the fact that there might be other valid forms of belief or other credible avenues of service. He was disposed to deny any other form of Christianity.

But John was changed. From Jesus he learned how wrong it was to label as false the faith of another because it was different from his own. His horizons were pushed back. He lost his air of superiority, overcame his feeling of self-righteousness. After Jesus' Resurrection, he placed his hands on the heads of new Samaritan converts, preached to the Gentiles, preserved for antiquity the prayer of our Lord, ". . . that they may be one even as we are one" (John 17:11), and put his stamp of approval upon the ministry of Paul. As the moonlight transforms the wayside puddle into a silvery pond, the sunlight of God transformed John into a tolerant and openminded person.

Saint Jerome illustrates this transformation by relating the story of John's preaching in the church at Ephesus. John was an old man, perhaps the only living person who had known Jesus in His physical life. News of his coming was widely publicized and on the appointed day a great crowd assembled. Every available space in the church and the area around it was filled.

When John arrived, he was so feeble he had to be carried into the place of worship. After eloquent words of welcome and a lengthy preparatory service, he was lifted to his feet to speak. A great hush came over the congregation. Everyone strained to hear each word. With deep conviction but shaky voice, he said, "Little children, love one another! Love one another!" This was all he said, but it was enough.

In a day of discussion and schism in the Christian community, when we cannot celebrate the Lord's Supper together or agree on the proper mode of baptism, *love* is a word we long to hear. How desperate is our need to care for one another! Tolerance and respect for other persons are more highly valued in the eyes of God than bias and sanctimony.

Then, too, John is a worthy person for young people to emulate because he learned that giving is always better than getting. Remember the day he joined his brother James in asking Jesus, "Grant us to sit, one at your right hand and one at your left, in your glory" (Mark 10:37). Evidently John considered Jesus a political Messiah who was going to Jerusalem to establish a visible kingdom. Feeling competent, he wanted to assure himself a chief place in the administration of that new government. It was as if he had become a disciple for the same reason many of us unite with the church, to see how much he could get out of it.

The request was selfish, greedy, and immature. Jesus sternly rebuked him for it. Greatness in the secular world, He said, is not like greatness in the Kingdom of God. In the secular world, the man is great who can compel others to serve him, but in the Kingdom of God greatness is measured by man's capacity to serve. "For even the Son of man came not to be ministered unto, but to minister, and to give his life a ransom for many" (Mark 10:45 KJV).

Love that is hoarded, moulds at last until we know some day
The only thing we ever have is what we give away.
And kindness that is never used but hidden all alone
Will slowly harden till it is as hard as any stone.
It is the things we always hold that we will lose some day;
The only things we ever keep are what we give away.

LOUIS GINSBURG

If John did not come to this realization the day he asked for preferment in the Kingdom of God, he did a few days later in the Upper Room when Jesus girded himself with a towel, stooped down and washed the disciples' feet. ". . . I have given you an example, [He said,] that you also should do as I have done to you. . . . a servant is not greater than his master. . . . If you know these things, blessed are you if you do them" (John 13:15–17).

From that very day, John devoted himself to the alleviation of human suffering and the fulfillment of others' needs. He offered his spiritual resources to all kinds and sorts and conditions of men. So gracious was his spirit, so devoted was he to the cause of Christ that the church at Ephesus elevated him to the office of Bishop. Giving, he learned, in the final analysis is always better than getting.

Finally, John is a worthy person for young people to emulate because he discovered that sacrificial love is the most powerful redemptive force in the world. One day as Jesus and the disciples were passing through Samaria, they approached a village where they hoped to spend the night. In those days, most of the Jews held the Samaritans in contempt and would have nothing to do with them. Sometimes the feeling was mutual. When Jesus and His disciples reached the village and the Samaritans learned they were bound for Jerusalem, no satisfactory lodging could be procured. Have you ever stopped at a motel after traveling hard all day and had the manager tell you there is no vacancy? It is hard to take. But what if you knew he had space and wouldn't let you have it because he didn't like your looks, or the color of your skin? It would get your dander up. This is what happened to John. The rebuff of the Samaritans gave rise to the angry question, "Lord, do you want us to bid fire come down from heaven and consume them?" (Luke 9:54). The scene reflects a mood that is prevalent in the civil-rights movement of our own time, particularly the black-power element whose philosophy is "Burn, baby, burn!"

Jesus soundly reprimanded the disciples. He told them it was not right to entertain such evil thoughts, that violence and vengeance have no place in the Christian life. Then He led them on to another village where they spent the night.

It was another lesson John did not soon forget. Two wrongs

do not make a right. Prejudiced Samaritans could not be won to the Kingdom by prejudiced disciples. Reconciliation is not possible so long as there is hatred and revenge in the heart. Love is the only sensible redemptive force in the world.

How well he learned is apparent in a story told by Clement of Alexandria. In a city of Ephesus, John met a young man who was strong of body, beautiful in appearance, and warm of heart. They became fast friends. When John left the city, he publicly commended the youth to the resident bishop for pastoral care. The bishop accepted the trust and pledged himself to it. He took the young man into his own home, treated him like a son, and eventually baptized him. Time passed and the bishop began to relax his care and vigilance. The young man fell into the wrong company and learned the ways of a thief. Soon the mountains, not the church, came to be his home. Then one day the youth decided that since he had drifted beyond the mercy of God, he would organize his own band of thieves.

Later John returned to the city and inquired about the youthful convert. In great embarrassment the bishop had to report, "He is dead."

"How and by what death?" John inquired.

"He had died to God," was the reply. Then the bishop told him how the youth had slipped from grace and had become a robber chieftain.

John rent his clothes. "A fine guardian of our brother's soul it was that I left!" he said. "But, now, let a horse be furnished for me, and let someone show me the way." So with horse and guide he rode straight from the church to find the youth. Approaching the headquarters of the robber band, he was captured and taken immediately to the leader. When the young man recognized John, he was smitten with shame and fled from his presence. Forgetting his old age, John pursued him. "Why do you flee from me, my child," he said, "from your own father, unarmed and old? Pity me, child, have no fear. You still have hope of life. I shall give an account for you to Christ. If need be, I will willingly endure your death, just as the Lord died for us. I shall give up my life for you. Stop! Believe! Christ has sent me!" The robber threw away his weapons and, weeping bitterly, fell into the arms of the aged apostle who restored him with tenderness to the fellowship of the church. Temper, yes! John still had a sharp tongue, but now it was softened by the spirit of Jesus Christ, disciplined by a passionate concern for others. He had learned that the greatest redemptive force is not violence or vengeance but sacrificial love.

It was a long way from the fishing boat of Capernaum to the dazzling heights of glory. It was a long way from Son of Thunder to the Apostle of Love, but John traveled the distance as a true soldier of the Cross. I should be proud if the youth of today would decide to cultivate his friendship.

6

An Ordinary Man

One of my most treasured mementos is a parchment bearing signatures of the fifty charter members of Saint Andrew's Methodist Church, located in southwest Little Rock. It was presented to me in April, 1964, at a dinner meeting following the formal organization of that body into a new United Methodist Church. I mention it simply because Andrew is the member of Jesus' cabinet we are to consider in this chapter.

Andrew was an ordinary fellow, a simple businessman who, with his brother Simon, operated a small fishing boat out of Bethsaida on the Sea of Galilee. Tradition says that while he was a large man and physically strong, he was slightly stooped. This is understandable. In all probability, he began work with his father at a very early age. Launching fishing boats was heavy work and pulling in nets, laden as they so often were with fish, was a man-size job. His young shoulders became slightly rounded as he gave himself year in and year out to the laborious task of fishing.

We know, too, that Andrew was a disciple of John the Baptist. Through this relationship, he became acquainted with Jesus. There was considerable speculation among the followers of John that the long-awaited Messiah was coming and that His coming would be soon. This expectation made John the Baptist's call to repentance sound a note of urgency. Then one day it came to pass. Israel's highest hope was realized. "I baptize with water; [John said,] but among you stands one whom you do not know, even he who comes after me, the thong of whose sandal I am not worthy to untie" (John 1:26, 27). He had been given the ability to note the presence of God's special gift to the world, to recognize Jesus as the Messiah. The next day John baptized Him in the river Jordan. There is no way of knowing if Andrew heard this testimony or witnessed this historic baptism, but it was through Andrew's relationship with John that he became acquainted with Jesus. Andrew and another disciple who must have been John, the son of Zebedee, were standing with him, John the Baptist, one day when Jesus appeared. As He walked by, John pointed Him out and said, "Behold, the Lamb of God!" (John 1:36). This first face-to-face encounter found them embarrassed and frustrated. They did not know how to act or what to say. All they could think to ask was, "Where do you live, Rabbi?" (John 1:38 TEV). Jesus answered, "Come and see" (John 1:39). It was a warm and gracious invitation, one which Andrew and his friend readily accepted. They spent the rest of the day with Jesus.

What happened during that visit no one knows. There is no record of their conversation, but Andrew came away from it profoundly convinced that Jesus was the Christ. He went at once to his brother Simon and said, "We have found the Messiah" (John 1:41). The experience of that day opened up a whole new way of life and Andrew was obviously excited about it. The occasion marked the beginning of a long and intimate association in the cabinet of our Lord.

First, consider Andrew's mind. What did he think about? What was his attitude? For one thing, he was filled with questions. All Andrew had ever known was fishing. It was a family trade which in typical Oriental fashion had been handed down from generation to generation. And, like so many of the young people in our world today, he was not completely satisfied with it as a way of life. He was restless, curious, given to the pursuit of a better way. He wanted to be freed from the shackles of his past, to be liberated from the prison of his own fears and anxieties. I can imagine that in those quiet moments of youthful contemplation he often said to himself (and here I use the contemporary language of Hermann Hagedorn):

> Lift up the curtain; for an hour lift up,
> The veil that holds your prisoners in this world
> Of coins and wires and motor-horns, this world
> Of figures and of men who trust in facts
> This pitiable, hypocritic world
> Where men with blinkered eyes and hobbled feet
> Grope down a narrow gorge and call it life.
>
> HERMANN HAGEDORN

Andrew wanted the curtain raised so that he might have the opportunity to discover who he was, why he was here, and where he was going. I say this because, as a disciple of John the Baptist, he traveled all the way from Bethsaida to Bethany (which in that day was no small distance) simply to ask about life's ultimate meaning and purpose. I say this, too, because he left every material thing to follow One who evidently answered his questions in a way that made sense. Andrew "took his mind out and danced on it, because he knew it was getting all caked up." His doubts proved a worthy discipline. They led him to Jesus Christ and to a life of great joy and personal satisfaction. Then, too, the mind of this young and dynamic disciple was given to the pursuit of positive and affirmative thoughts. He was an incurable optimist.

"While climbing a great cliff one day, two boys found a nest of eagle eggs. They put the eggs under a hen in the barnyard, and in due time the young eagles hatched with the chicks and the mother hen cared for them as though they were her own. One day a great eagle swooped down over the barnyard and saw the young eagles on the ground. The young eagles, feeling kinship to the great eagle, tried their wings, found that they, too, could fly. Day after day the great eagle came. Day after day the young eagles tried their wings. Then one day the young eagles flew high in the air and followed the great eagle into the limitless sky, their native atmosphere."

This anecdote, as told by Gaston Foote in *Footnotes*, illustrates Andrew's nature. He was like that great eagle. He knew man's native atmosphere is far beyond anything we have yet attained, that imprisoned within us are boundless possibilities waiting to be released.

When he looked into the eyes of Jesus, he saw mirrored there, not his shortcomings and inadequacies, but the image of the man God intended him to be. Then he thought of his brother, how his aggressive personality and natural leadership ability could be used to good advantage in building the Kingdom of God.

The role which he played in the feeding of the five thousand is also expressive of this tendency to think positively (*see* John 6:1–15). It was late in the day. The people were tired and hungry. There was no food to distribute. The disciples were discussing the situation among themselves when Andrew appeared. With him was a little boy who had in his hands five barley loaves and two fish. He presented the boy to Jesus. Jesus took the boy's lunch, blessed it and divided it among the people. There was more than enough for all. It is significant that the boy was willing to share his food, but it is more significant that it was Andrew who brought him to Jesus. He alone among the disciples was sensitive to the possibilities hidden deep within the boy and concealed in his lunch box. Not only this, he demonstrated utmost confidence in Jesus' ability to use what the boy had to offer to feed the multitude.

Lord Thomas Sewer has said that the human mind is like a parachute, it functions only when open. Andrew's mind was always open, not just to questions about life's ultimate meaning, but to the full potentiality of our manhood.

Secondly, consider the spirit of this young and dynamic disciple. How did he act? What role did he play? He was most assuredly an evangelist. Each time Andrew is mentioned in the New Testament he is introducing someone to Jesus. First, it was his brother Simon. There is no more difficult place to begin witnessing than among the members of one's own immediate family. The relationship is too intimate, too familiar. It is much easier to talk about spiritual matters to strangers, but for Andrew the missionary causes began where it ought always to begin—in the home.

The next person he brought to Jesus was a little boy. There were hundreds of people that day who overlooked the presence of children. Those who recognized them at all probably thought them a nuisance, a hindrance, a worry, and a care. Not Andrew. He loved children and had a special interest in boys. That day he had befriended at least one—perhaps he interpreted Jesus' message for him. When the opportunity was presented, he took advantage of it, came to Jesus and said, "There is a lad here . . ." (John 6:9). Think of the way of life that introduction opened up for this boy. Oh, how he must have thrilled at that moment! We don't know what happened to him after the feeding of the five thousand, but with some degree of authority, we can imagine he became a tower of strength in the growth and expansion of the early Christian community.

The third group of people whom Andrew introduced to Jesus were total strangers. They were Greeks who had come to Jerusalem with Jewish friends for the Feast of the Passover (*see* John 12:20–22). They first made their request of Philip. But Philip was unsure of the Gentiles place in the Kingdom so he turned the matter over to Andrew who immediately took them to Jesus. He would not keep any man from seeing his Lord simply because he was a Gentile.

Andrew was not an eloquent public speaker. Certainly he was not as powerful a pulpiteer as his brother Simon. But in his own quiet and unassuming way, he made it a regular practice to introduce men to Jesus. Andrew's spirit was that of a true evangelist. It was as if he had prayed:

> Show me the way, not to fortune and fame,
> Not how to win laurels or praise for my name —
> But Show Me The Way to spread "The Great Story"
> That "Thine is The Kingdom and Power and Glory."
>
> HELEN STEINER RICE

Andrew also played the role of second fiddle. He was the first disciple to be called, but he was never included in that intimate inner circle. It was always James, Peter, and John who were with Jesus in His great and most dramatic moments. There were times when Andrew was on the fringe, but he was never really a vital part of that executive committee. Then, too, the New Testament writers invariably identified Andrew as Simon Peter's brother. It is never easy to bask in the reflected glory of a more illustrious person, especially when that person happens to be a member of one's own family.

It punctures a man's ego when he is constantly shoved into the background, when he is always assigned a minor role, when his name is never called the night awards are distributed. Still, Andrew played the part with a rare and impeccable grace.

In June, 1863, when Lee invaded Pennsylvania, a distinguished citizen of Philadelphia wired General Henry Wagner Halleck, Chief of Staff in Washington, offering his services. He received this brusque reply: "We have five times as many generals as we know what to do with, but are greatly in need of privates."

The need for leadership is the same in the army of our Lord. There are many who want the spotlight, the notoriety, the reward, but there are few who are willing to become cheerfully involved in the mundane chores of living and serving. In this respect Andrew was a private. As long as the work was done, he did not care who received the credit. His was a self-effacing humility. He was perfectly content with second place. Lance Webb said that to be big in spirit even though one's capacity is small, is to be great. That kind are the backbone of the church. They have jobs to do and do them without complaint. Such was the character of Andrew.

Finally, consider the fruit of Andrew's ministry. What did he achieve? How effective was his witness? The name of Sir Wilfred Grenfell will not soon be forgotten. He was a great medical doctor who gave himself to the poor and neglected fishermen of Labrador, but who today remembers that Dwight L. Moody brought him to Christ? Only a few. Billy Graham is one of the spiritual giants in today's world, but how many know the man under whose ministry he was converted? Not many. Yet these insignificant men live on because the shadow of their influence fell upon those who were destined for greatness. So Andrew. What a void would have been felt in the early Christian community had he not introduced his brother to Jesus! As Dr. Claude McKay has said, "There would have been no eloquent Peter at Pentecost had there been no humble Andrew to bring him to Jesus." This was his greatest contribution to the church.

There is an encouraging word here. No one can know what one ordinary life dedicated to God can do to bless the world. No scales are sufficiently delicate to record the weight of the unconscious influence of a single life. God is able to multiply our talent, however insignificant it may be, when that talent is offered to Him.

Furthermore, tradition reports that Andrew traveled far and wide as an itinerant preacher visiting such lands as Macedonia, Greece, Turkey, and even Russia, and that he was martyred in A.D. 69. There is a beautiful story about those last days of his life. In Patros of Achaia, Greece, the lovely Maximillia, wife of the proconsul, was converted under his ministry. This angered the proconsul and led him to order Andrew beaten and then crucified on a huge cross shaped like an X, which from that day has been called Crux decussata, or St. Andrew's cross. He hung two days on the cross preaching to the people and praising God. It is said that Maximillia later claimed Andrew's body and lovingly buried it in her own tomb. In the fifth century, Saint Regalus is said to have carried his bones to Scotland and to have founded a city which bears his name. Thus the ordinary life of Andrew had an extraordinary reach.

7

The Tax Collector

The life story of many great men can rightly be divided into two parts—before and after. On the Damascus Road a transformation of such magnitude took place in Saul of Tarsus that his life can best be studied in terms of before and after that dramatic event.

There came at last in the life of Saint Augustine a moment when the prayers of his Christian mother caught up with him. He was converted. The miraculous bestowal of God's grace effected such a radical change in conduct and concern that his life can easily be calculated in terms of before and after that stellar moment.

One night in a little chapel off Aldersgate Street, London, England, John Wesley felt his heart strangely warmed. The experience was a miniature Pentecost. It produced a new man. Whereas he had been only a seeker after truth, now he was an evangelist set on fire for the truth as he understood it. Aldersgate marked the continental divide in the life of the founder of the Methodist Church.

This before and after principle can also be applied to the

disciple Matthew. To adequately appreciate his contribution to Christianity, we have to ask the same two questions: What kind of person was he prior to Christ's call to discipleship and what kind of person did he become upon accepting this gracious invitation?

We know very little about Matthew. The central figure in the New Testament is Jesus. The writers were so preoccupied with His life and ministry that Matthew and others who followed Him were often pushed aside or taken for granted. Still there are a few facts that can be gleaned from the Scriptures and from tradition. Matthew is also known as Levi, the name given him by both Mark and Luke. He was a native of Galilee. His home was in or about Capernaum, one of the most important cities in the gospels and a principal thoroughfare in the ancient world. Roads through the city led from Damascus to Jerusalem and on to Egypt and continued from all points leading to the Mediterranean. All moving armies and significant caravans laden with passengers and freight bound for distant points passed that way. Capernaum was a major trade center strategically located on the Sea of Galilee. It was a most lucrative place for a customs official to do business.

Matthew was an educated man, perhaps the most learned member of Jesus' cabinet. How else can we explain his shrewd business sense, his uncanny ability to keep an accurate record of what must have been a complicated tax system, his skill in compiling an account of Jesus' life and work? Along the way Matthew must have received some formal training in the basic rudiments of education—reading, writing, and arithmetic.

Furthermore, he was ambitious and self-seeking, determined to get rich, to be successful no matter how great the cost. Matthew was a publican, a customs official, an agent of the internal revenue department of Rome whose job was to collect a certain amount of taxes for the government—an attractive position because it was so lucrative. All monies collected over and above the authorized levy could be retained by the tax collector, and he could legally collect as much money as his ingenuity and resourcefulness would permit. He could even take all of a man's property as payment for taxes and get by with it. As William P. Barker has so succinctly stated: "Anything they collected above that amount was pure gravy for them. And how the publicans loved that gravy!" With such a high rate of return on his investment, Matthew had sufficient resources to pay for his political office (it was a common practice for men to advance rather sizable sums to gain the position of tax collector) and at the same time live luxuriously.

To the government, Matthew's job was important. Insofar as taxes were concerned, his word was law. Men obeyed his commands. Those whose goods had to pass under his inspection were careful to win and hold his goodwill. We have every reason to believe that, in the beginning at least, Matthew thoroughly enjoyed the status, the power, and the civil authority invested in him by Rome.

However, what success Matthew achieved in this office was gained at great cost to himself. All publicans and tax collectors were hated and despised. The Romans abhorred them for their corruption and treachery. It is said that Tacitus, a second-century historian whose writings were extremely critical of the Roman emperors, once erected a statue to an honest tax collector, a fact that speaks forcefully of the dishonesty of the usual men in this political office. The Jews loathed them for their betrayal of the country. To be a tax collector under normal circumstances is bad enough, but to collect taxes from one's own people and then pay these taxes to an alien power is inexcusable. Yet this was a publican's profession. So far as the Jews were concerned, they were enemy agents, collaborators, traitors, men who had sold their own souls and their native land down the river for personal gain.

No wonder Matthew's word was worthless in the courts! No wonder men shunned him and made him feel unwelcome at social functions! No wonder his money was unacceptable in the synagogue! All tax collectors were considered reprobates and were classified with the harlots and sinners. No one ever showed concern about their problems.

In the loneliness of this estrangement, Matthew must have asked himself a thousand times if he had made a good bargain. He may have started out right; he may have had good intentions and the purest of motives. But the stench of the office got to him and dragged him down to the gutter along with his fellow publicans.

Surely he must have been looking for a way out. There is no way of knowing for sure, but we have good reason to believe Matthew's dissatisfaction caused him to turn to the Scriptures. Then news came of John the Baptist. He was preaching, "Repent, for the kingdom of heaven is at hand. . . . Prepare the way of the Lord, make his paths straight" (Matthew 3:2, 3). Matthew's heart must have been quickened by the realization that he was living in the days of fulfilled prophecy. He had been ruled out of the synagogue, but John welcomed publicans. He had been condemned as an outcast, but here was a man who criticized the respected religious leaders of the day—the Scribes and Pharisees. Surely this encouraged him to seek more diligently God's plan for his life. The passage, which promised the coming of a Messiah who would redeem Israel, gave him hope.

Then Jesus appeared with a message far more beautiful

than anything he had read or heard, and Capernaum became headquarters for this Galilean ministry! Since his own seat of customs was located on one of the city's thoroughfares, it is very likely that they rubbed shoulders. Surely their paths must have crossed. Can't you visualize him listening as the Master spoke in parables, watching as He performed miracles? Under Jesus' ministry the hopeless found hope, the sick were made well, the blind to see. It was good news to an outcast publican like Matthew.

One day Jesus stopped at his tax office, looked him in the eye and said, "Follow me" (Matthew 9:9). Matthew arose and followed Him. There was no quibbling about the sacrifice it entailed, no stalling for time to think the matter over. It was a straight from the shoulder invitation and an honest affirmative answer.

The occasion marked the beginning of a whole new life. Matthew no longer spent his energy producing revenue for Rome and for his own greedy purse. Now he labored for the distribution of wealth. He thought about the needs of others. He shared his resources. His whole life was devoted to the building of spiritual values.

The first thing he did as a disciple was to throw a great banquet for his fellow outcasts. It was an imaginative way to announce his newfound faith and, at the same time, give his friends a chance to see and hear the Lord. No one knows what happened that night, but we can be sure that many lives were touched by Jesus' forgiving love and persuasive influence.

However, the affair was viewed with strong disapproval by the Scribes and the Pharisees. It gave them another opportunity to criticize Jesus for associating with those who they felt were unworthy of spiritual favors. "Why does your teacher eat with tax collectors and sinners?" they cried (Matthew 9:11). But these were the people Jesus loved.

"Those who are well have no need of a physician, [He said,] but those who are sick. . . . I came not to call the righteous, but sinners" (Matthew 9:12, 13).

What happened to Matthew following that dinner meeting is a mystery. His name is listed among the apostles in the Book of Acts, indicating that he was loyal at least through the trials of the Crucifixion. But traditions regarding his subsequent ministry are confused. Many are fantastic legends. Here the student is confronted with a mass of hopeless contradictions. Nevertheless, by reading between the lines, it is clear that Matthew was a true apostle: He was one of the first to write down the teachings of Jesus; he became a missionary of the gospel and died a hero of the faith.

Never was there a more unpromising candidate for the ministry. Matthew was a disloyal Jew who had accumulated great wealth and it is "easier for a camel to go through the eye of a needle than for a rich man to enter the kingdom of God" (Luke 18:25). But in the hands of Christ, this unlikely material was melted, molded, and gloriously used for the building of the church. Before Christ called him to disciple-ship, Matthew was a shrewd, calculating businessman with no thought for anyone other than himself. But after accepting this gracious invitation, Matthew became an other-centered person whose primary objective was to give away the joy and peace which he had found.

We owe an enormous debt of gratitude to this young and dynamic disciple. He warns about the danger of orienting life around material values, tells that the doors of the church should be open to everyone, and calls attention to the fact that a personal relationship to Jesus Christ is the most im-portant single thing in the world. We shudder at the thought of what might have happened had he not accepted the call to discipleship. His life would have come to no good end. But Matthew did and his whole life was transformed.

Paul Quillian in *Not a Sparrow Falls* tells about Sir Philip Bridges, the organist at Saint Paul's Cathedral in London, who was out on a walking tour through the countryside. One evening he came to a village church and asked the sexton if he might have the privilege of playing the organ. The sexton, noticing his modest demeanor and his cultured speech, thought surely it would be fitting for a stranger like that to have that privilege, so he gave him the key. As Bridges slipped into the church and seated himself at the organ, the sexton remained in the vestibule; presently strains such as he had never heard before poured forth under the skilled fingers of that marvelous musician. When Bridges closed the organ and came out through the vestibule and handed him back the key, the sexton looked at him with awestruck eyes and said, "Sir, I never knew our organ could produce music like that."

Matthew did not know the organ of his life would produce great music, that it was capable of begetting stereophonic sound. He was completely oblivious of the fact that it could effect beauty and harmony, but he found out. When fingers of the living Christ played upon the keyboard of his heart, Matthew discovered that everything Jesus touches is lifted to a higher level, ennobled, and glorified.

8

The Altogether Human

I attended the Annual Girl Scout Taster's Tea with my daughter. When the mistress of ceremonies mentioned with much affection and appreciation the name of Lady Baden Powell, I was somehow reminded of the importance which men have given to beginnings. Consider George Washington's birthday. It is a national holiday not because he was *a* president of the United States, but because he was *the first* president of the United States. Most civic clubs and fraternal groups have sometime during the year what they call a Founder's Day program. Generally, they are solemn occasions when those who gave birth to their organization are remembered in some special way. In this chapter, we consider a man who should hold just such an honored place in our hearts—Philip of Bethsaida. As one of the chosen Twelve, he is numbered among the founders of the Christian Church. You might say he was a charter member of the oldest and most famous fishing club in the world, an exclusive fellowship open to anyone who accepts Jesus' invitation to become fishers of men.

Philip was a country boy from northern Galilee, the fifth

member of Jesus' cabinet to be selected from the little fishing village of Bethsaida. Like Andrew, his name was Greek, though we have every reason to believe he was a devout Jew. When interpreted from the Greek, *Philip* means lover of horses, which has given rise to the tradition that he might have been an expert horseman and a charioteer among the Romans who occupied the garrisons of his community. But, being from Bethsaida, he is far more likely to have been a simple fisherman.

We must be careful to distinguish him from another Philip mentioned in the Book of Acts. This second Philip was one of the seven who were chosen by the apostles to serve the tables (*see* Acts 6:5). He conducted a successful missionary campaign in Samaria (*see* Acts 8:5–14), he was the means of the conversion of the Ethiopian eunuch (*see* Acts 8:26–40), and he occasionally entertained Paul in his home at Caesarea (*see* Acts 21:8); but he was not a member of Jesus' cabinet. Even though Tertullain and Eusebius (and many other reliable authorities on the early church) confused the two Philips, we must not fall into this same error. Most modern scholars lead us to believe they were two different persons.

What then can we say with integrity? Is there anything we can know for sure about Philip of Bethsaida?

First, he was altogether human. For instance, he was shy and retiring. In the four incidents recorded of him in the New Testament, three times he is sought out by others. Andrew and his friend looked for Jesus, but Jesus "found Philip and said to him, 'Follow me' " (John 1:43). The same fact comes to light in the feeding of the five thousand. When the multitudes pressed about Him, Jesus sought Philip and asked him, "How are we to buy bread, so that these people may eat?" (John 6:5). Philip knew at once the resources that were available, but he had to be sought out before his opinion was given.

When the Greeks came up to Jerusalem for the Passover, they came to Philip with the request, "Sir, we wish to see Jesus" (John 12:21). Once again the initiative was taken by someone else.

No doubt some of you who read these lines would like to render a special service to the church or to carry out some creative activity to help build the Kingdom of God. But instead of stepping forward and announcing this interest, you just sit quietly and wait for someone to knock on your door or call you on the telephone. This was Philip. He was a man of solid worth and strong character, but he was not aggressive. It was almost as though he were reluctant to become intimately involved in the work and witness of Jesus Christ.

He was slow to make up his mind on major issues. When Jesus called him to discipleship, Philip withheld his answer until he had an opportunity to talk it over with his closest friend, Nathanael. Only after carefully calculating the cost did he join the apostolic band. When the Greeks came to him with their request to see Jesus, his immediate reaction was to recoil from the decision that was thrust upon him. It was not until after consulting with Andrew that Philip consented to give the Greeks an audience with his Lord.

How many times have you heard people say, "Nothing is harder for me than making up my mind!" Such was the case with Philip. He was not given to hasty decisions.

He was practical, matter-of-fact, and unimaginative. When Jesus asked how to feed the multitude, Philip said it was an impossible task. He had obviously studied the problem carefully: "Lord, we have only forty dollars and that won't buy food for five thousand people" (*see* John 6:7). His analytical mind told him the multitude simply could not be fed with the available resources.

Have you ever been on a board when a challenging and far-reaching program was presented and some member of the board, noting that only X-number of dollars were available, said it couldn't be done? His kind are modern Philips. We need them in our churches. They know well the value of a dollar and help to keep us solvent. But we also need some Andrews. Philip with his cold and calculating mind said, "It is impossible." Andrew with his firm faith in Jesus said, "Here is the way it can be done." Had it not been for him the five thousand would have not been fed. Philip was a man of practical common sense. His thoughts moved on the dead level of literal fact.

He found belief difficult. For this reason, some scholars have called him a dullard. In the Upper Room discourse Jesus told the disciples about His relationship to God: "I am the way, and the truth and the life. . . . If you had known me, you would have known my Father also; henceforth you know him and have seen him" (John 14:6, 7). Philip was either not listening attentively or he did not understand. He asked, "Lord, show us the Father, and we shall be satisfied" (John 14:8).

The question expresses a universal yearning. We all should like to have a special revelation, something that would make us certain of God, but faith seldom comes this way. Belief is hard.

Finally—and I think commendably—Philip did on occasion exercise good judgment. That he did not always do so, as we have seen, is not a contradiction in his character but a demonstration of the complex nature of the human mind. After reporting to Nathanael that he had found the Messiah, and Nathanael had said somewhat sarcastically, "Can anything good come out of Nazareth?" Philip said to him, "Come and see" (John 1:46). He knew that men are not won by eloquent achievement, that the only real answer to propaganda is performance.

A little girl in the Crimea saw Florence Nightingale, the

angel of mercy, going from one sickbed to another bringing a triumphant smile and a word of good cheer to each wounded soldier. One day she asked Miss Nightingale, "Are you kin to Jesus?" Christianity became a vital force in this girl's life, not because she had worked her way through the maze of theological dogma or had engaged in serious debate, but because she had seen it demonstrated in a person.

So Philip. He invited his friend to discover for himself what he had seen with his own eyes. It was good judgment. His "come and see" approach to evangelism continues to be our most effective means of communicating the gospel.

Jesus chose twelve men to be His closest friends and helpers. Somehow, over the past 1,950 years we have turned them into supermen. We have clothed them with so much pious respect that we lose sight of them as human beings, but they were amazingly similar to us. Pick them out of the first century and drop them into the twentieth and they could be accepted as contemporaries. Take them out of Galilee and put them on any Main Street, U.S.A., and they would belong. The disciples were altogether human. This is especially true of Philip. He was shy and retiring, slow to make up his mind, practical and unimaginative, the kind of man who found faith difficult, yet who at times was capable of making sound judgments. His disposition and temperament were very much like our own, but Jesus selected him as a disciple nonetheless. Upon the recommendation of Andrew and Peter, He went to the place where Philip was, looked him in the eye and said, "Follow me" (John 1:43). This, despite his human weaknesses, despite his shortcomings and inadequacies.

During World War II Bishop Oxnan says he was asked to visit the battlefront. He had a son who was in the invasion of Anzio Beach. The plane the bishop was in flew over the beachhead. He said he looked down upon that costly bit of sand and it looked like a face that had suffered from smallpox.

Later, he walked over the sands with his son. His son said, "Dad, I will take you to my foxhole."

The Bishop said: "Nonsense, son, you can't find a particular foxhole on a beach like this."

To which the boy replied: "If you had been here for three and a half months you could find it." And they did.

The young man took a few pictures. Then he said to his father: "Dad, I want you to come with me to the cemetery."

They went to the cemetery. There are 9,500 crosses there. The young man took his bishop father to one particular cross and said: "Dad, would you say a prayer here?"

"Why here?" his father asked.

"Well, that's Danner. He was right beside me when he got his as we came ashore."

And so the bishop offered a prayer.

The young man who had known Danner had put a value on him. He was saying that Danner was a young man worth knowing — and now, worth remembering.

BEN F. LEHMBERG

Something of this same quality is evident here. Jesus put a value on Philip. He saw him as a man of worth. He sensed that he had the leadership capability which would make him useful in the circle of the Twelve. No wonder He gave him the status of a cabinet member!

The scene opens our minds to the fact that Christ can use men of every ability. In His eyes no one is unimportant or insignificant. He is perpetually optimistic about the soul of man. He sees us not for what we are, but for what by His grace we may become.

Two things happened to Philip as a result of his intimate association with Jesus. He grew, as did his Lord, "in wisdom and in stature, and in favor with God and man" (Luke 2:52), and he spent himself in selfless service. In the feeding of the five thousand, he discovered that little is much in the hands of Christ, that with God all things are possible. William A. McIntyre said in his book *Christ's Cabinet*, "When a man gives Christ loaves, He gives back more loaves. When a man gives Christ himself, Christ gives back a larger and finer self." We cannot live by visible, tangible, demonstrated facts alone. To make progress we must dare; we must walk by faith. This truth was impressed indelibly upon Philip's mind when Jesus multiplied the loaves and fish.

In the Upper Room, he learned that God is infinitely greater than the mind can comprehend, that He can only be seen through the eyes of faith, that the best way to know Him is to look into the face of Jesus. "Have I been with you so long, and yet you do not know me, Philip? He who has seen me has seen the Father. . . . Do you not believe that I am in the Father and the Father in me?" (John 14:9, 10). Here, he discovered, is man's clearest photograph of God.

The miracle of the story is that this altogether human, this intensely conservative man rose up and followed Jesus. Throwing all caution to the wind, he said:

> If Jesus Christ is a man —
> And only a man, — I say
> That of all mankind I cleave to him,
> And to him will I cleave alway.

> If Jesus Christ is a God —
> And the only God, — I swear

I will follow him through heaven and hell,
The earth, the sea, the air!

RICHARD WATSON GILDER

And Philip did! He became a radiant and effective witness to the good news of the gospel. He introduced Nathanael to Jesus. Together with Andrew he took the Greeks to see his Lord. Tradition further suggests that after the Ascension, he was one of the great lights of the church in Asia Minor and that he was martyred on a *T* cross at Hierapolis. After his death he was wrapped for burial in sheets of Syriac paper and papyrus reeds because he felt unworthy to be wrapped in linen as was his Lord. So to the very end Philip remained a loyal and faithful disciple.

9

The Disciple Who Became a Rock

A fascinating member of Jesus' cabinet was Simon Peter. The course of his life portrays a man's journey from shifting sand to solid rock, from humble fisherman to stalwart apostle. Historians refer to him as the impulsive, the impetuous, or the irresponsible one. Lloyd C. Douglas calls him The Big Fisherman. Others speak of him as the one who denied his Lord. To the disciples, he was the spokesman for the Twelve. To Jesus, he was the rock upon which He built His church. Taken singly none of these expressions is an adequate description. What then can we say about him? What words best depict Simon Peter?

One is *valiant*. From the beginning, Peter was a fearless disciple. Only a brave man will jeopardize his security by throwing himself without any preparation into a new and different way of life. The risk is too great. Yet, Peter did this. All he had ever known was fishing. The only thing he had done was sail his boat on the Sea of Galilee and draw from the waters that which when sold provided a livelihood for his family. Then one day Jesus appeared on the beach where he and his brother, Andrew, were working. He said to them, "Follow me, and I will make you fishers of men" (Matthew 4:19). There was something so irresistible and persuasive about the invitation, something so dynamic and compelling about the way it was extended, Peter could not say no. He did not plead for time to talk the matter over, to weigh the dangers, or to meditate upon the sacrifices it might entail. He simply accepted the invitation. Matthew says, "Immediately they left their nets and followed him" (Matthew 4:20). No weakling could have made this decision and so quickly turned his back on familiar things to follow a Stranger from Galilee.

A violent storm swept across the Sea of Galilee. It tossed the disciples' boat about like a toothpick. They were fearful for their lives. Then Jesus appeared walking on the water (*see* Matthew 14:22–33). Some shrank back in fear. "It is a ghost!" they cried. Peter said, "Lord, if it is You, bid me come to You on the water." Jesus replied, "Come." Unlike the others less valiant than he, Peter plunged right in. He was willing to risk his life walking on the water if Jesus said the word.

At Caesarea Philipi, Jesus essayed to evaluate his ministry (*see* Matthew 16:13–16). "Who do men say that I am?" He asked.

The disciples answered, "Some say John the Baptist, others say Elijah and others Jeremiah or one of the prophets."

He then inquired, "But who do you say that I am?"

Peter replied, "You are the Christ, the Son of the living God."

It was his confession of faith, a confession which later became the faith of the whole church. The explanation shows Peter as a man of courageous conviction, willing to speak what he thought and felt regardless of the consequences.

Distressed with the abrupt turn of events in the Garden of

Gethsemane, Peter drew a sword and cut off one of the soldier's ears (*see* John 18:10, 11). Granted it was a savage retort to Jesus' arrest, the feat was done in defense of his Lord. It was another manifestation of bravery in the midst of battle.

There are other examples. Suffice it to say, Peter proved himself to be a fearless disciple. He was a real man, a man's man — rough, rugged, and ready for any action necessary to advance the cause of Christ.

This is not the whole story. To the word *valiant* must be added the word *vacillating*. Peter was impulsive and impetuous, prone to leap before he looked. In the Upper Room, Jesus girded Himself with a towel and washed the disciples' feet (*see* John 13:1–10). Then Jesus explained how the spirit of humility was basic, that no one could be a true disciple without first being a servant of all. Withdrawal of Peter's feet would, in essence, signify his withdrawal from the teaching of the Master. Cognizant of this fact, he blurted out, "Lord, not my feet only, but also my hands and my head" (John 13:9). From one extreme to the other, that was Peter. He would not participate at all or he would require a whole bath.

Jesus had warned the disciples that they would fall away, but Peter laughed it off. "Though they all fall away because of you, [he said,] I will never fall away" (Matthew 26:33). Peter was dangerously sure of himself. Then, in another rash display of confidence, he said, "Even if I must die with you, I will not deny you" (Matthew 26:35).

The next day Jesus was arrested. As predicted, the disciples began to fall away but not Peter. He was anxious to know what was going to happen so he followed at a distance and through the courtesy of an unnamed disciple gained admittance into the courtyard of the high priest's home. There the contradiction materialized. When the fire which had been kindled suddenly blazed up, lighting the faces of those who huddled about it, he was recognized. A maid approached him and said, "You also were with Jesus the Galilean" (Matthew 26:69). He denied it, and twice more within the hour swore he did not know the Man. Then the cock crowed. Luke adds, "The Lord turned and looked at Peter" (Luke 22:61). In that moment Peter's heart was awakened, his arrogance and conceit shattered. He was the same vacillating and unstable disciple he had always been.

Note further his role in the establishment of the church. Remarkably, during his early ministry, Paul persuaded Peter to liberalize his strict Hebraic tendencies. As a matter of fact, at the Jerusalem Conference these two established Christian leaders agreed that Gentile converts could join the church without circumcision (that is, without submitting to the ceremonial laws of the synagogue). But under the influence of the strict Judaistic party of Jerusalem, Peter reversed himself. Former restraints of narrow legalism took hold of him. He began to withdraw fellowship from the uncircumcised Gentiles. When the breach was complete, Paul had to rebuke him for this backward step: "But when Cephas [Peter] came to Antioch I opposed him to his face, because he stood condemned" (Galatians 2:11). Peter's wobbly theological fluctuations gave rise to much confusion within the community of faith.

Little wonder the early church fathers called him *Petra* meaning little stones! Small, smooth, shifting pebbles are never a good foundation upon which to build either a house or a life. Yet the name was quite appropriate for one of Peter's changing disposition.

The last word we shall use to describe Peter is *victorious*. No matter how many times he fell, he always got up. No matter how many mistakes he made, he tried again. No matter how often he failed, still he pressed on toward the goal of fellowship with his Lord and his God. Such persistence is never without reward.

Peter's first step toward victory came on Easter morning. The women had gone to the garden to care for the body of Jesus. They wished to anoint it with fragrant oils and spices. But the tomb was empty. An angel spoke to them, "He has risen, he is not here; see the place where they laid him. But go, tell his disciples and Peter . . ." (Mark 16:6, 7). How this must have thrilled Peter's heart! Jesus had explicitly called him by name. It was as if He had said, "Peter, your sins are forgiven. I believe in you. I am depending on you to build My church." Now, a man will do almost anything to prove himself worthy of the trust and confidence placed in him by another. This is what Peter did. He lived up to the nickname given to him by Jesus.

The second step occurred a few days later. The fishermen among the disciples had returned to their nets. They had toiled all night and caught nothing. As dawn approached, they saw the figure of a solitary Man on the shore. He instructed them to "cast the net on the right side of the boat" (John 21:6). They did and snared more fish than their boat would hold. John whispered to Peter, "It is the Lord!" (John 21:7). Peter, in characteristic fashion, plunged into the cold waters to greet his Master.

When they had finished breakfast, Jesus said to him, "Simon, son of John, do you love me more than these?" He replied, "Yes Lord; you know that I love you" (John 21:15, 16). Three times the question was asked and the answer given. In each instance Jesus said to him, "Tend my sheep." It was his way of telling Peter to roll up his sleeves and go to work, that men everywhere might know of the risen Christ.

This Peter did with great effectiveness. At Pentecost, he preached with such boldness and power that three thousand souls were baptized and received into the church (*see* Acts 2:40, 41). At the council of the high priest, he declared his faith with such courage men recognized that he had been with Jesus. He said, "Whether it is right in the sight of God to listen to you rather than to God, you must judge; for we cannot but speak of what we have seen and heard" (Acts 4:19, 20). Thus possessed by the Holy Spirit, Peter pushed out into new areas of paganism where he proclaimed the gospel of the risen Christ with telling results.

There is a legend that Peter arrived in Rome amid a tidal wave of Christian persecutions. When he saw men and women being burned to death, being devoured by hungry lions, his first impulse was to run away, to flee for his life. Outside the city gates he met a man carrying a cross. He asked him, "*Quo Vadis?*" (Whither thou goest?) The man replied, "I am going to Rome to be crucified with my Lord." Peter turned in his tracks. He was no more Simon *Petra* (little stones), but Simon *Petros* (a solidified rock of strength). He had made his last retreat. He was crucified just as his Lord was crucified, but insisted on being nailed to the cross head downward. He felt unworthy to imitate his Master in that final hour. Such is the portrait of the chief of disciples, endowed with valiance, spotted with vacillation, crowned with victory.

10

An Insurrectionist Turned Disciple

There were among the disciples of Jesus two Simons — Simon Peter and Simon the Zealot. The latter was as obscure as the first was prominent. Except for the four listings of the Twelve Apostles, we know nothing about him other than his name. However, despite this limited knowledge, we can make some reasonable assumptions about his nature and person.

For instance, the descriptive phrase, the Zealot, attached to his name tells of the friends with whom he ran. A typical Jewish patriot, Simon was disturbed by the aggressive and domineering yoke of Rome. In this respect, he was like the citizens of some of the younger nations of the world who once suffered at the hands of a foreign power. In bondage they cried out as did one of our own forefathers, Patrick Henry, "Is life so dear or peace so sweet as to be purchased at the price of chains and slavery? Forbid it, Almighty God! I know not what course others may take, but as for me, give me liberty or give me death." In the past fifteen years, we have seen many of these underprivileged people gain political freedom. They have become independent and their representatives are now members in full standing of the United Nations General Assembly. Such exactly was the dream of Simon the Zealot. He wanted his people to be free of the political pressures of Rome, and Israel restored to its rightful place among the kingdoms of the world.

It was a worthy cause, but in his pursuit of it Simon fell under the influence of a few hotheaded radicals who used the ideal to justify their bitterness and violence. Most of the Jews had become more or less resigned to their fate and had agreed to live as best they could with their oppressors. Some of them —notably the publicans—had even started to work for the Romans collecting their taxes, but not this band of renegade vigilantes to whom Simon had become attached! The Zealots, as they were called, would plunder and destroy at the slightest provocation. They would sabotage every plan of Rome. They would deliberately burn the property of any Sadducee, priest, or publican who was known to be a collaborator with Rome. They would as easily thrust their daggers into the bowels of a Jewish friend of Rome as into those of a Roman soldier. As one Methodist bishop has noted, "They talked a good deal about brotherhood, but along the way they dropped the brother and kept the hood." The Zealots were a terrible lot, a seething underground movement with a deep-seated commitment to overthrow the government.

Every now and then, usually under cover of night, these guerrilla fighters would strike. It was always like a volcano erupting. In the wake of these warlike attacks, they would leave only the dirty stench of smoke and blood. One can almost hear them saying: "We have no God but Jehovah; we give no taxes but to the Temple; we have no friends but a Zealot." It was a philosophy that provoked their use of power and force. But ironically, the philosophy held the seed for the destruction of their own ideal. One historian succinctly stated that the Zealots left a tragic picture. Their zeal consumed friend more effectively than foe; their fires left Jewish homes in ashes, but Rome unhurt by the flame. Their irrational revolt brought death and destruction to those they would make free. Their love of country destroyed the very country they loved.

Simon was a Jewish patriot, but he turned into a fanatic, became a rebel, an insurrectionist, and a murderer. This is a reasonable assumption because of the descriptive phrase attached to his name. A man is known by the company he keeps.

We can also infer something about the character of this dynamic disciple because he fell under the influence of Jesus Christ. We don't know why or how it happened. It may have been that Simon saw in Jesus a possible replacement for the leader of the Zealot movement who had fallen in the heat of battle a few years previously. It may have been that he was disappointed in the political reforms made possible through the Zealot movement and was giving some second thoughts to his involvement with such radical revolutionaries. It may have been that he was simply impressed with the work and witness of Jesus. After all, He was doing more for Israel than the violent Zealots would or could ever hope to do. He was transforming lives and effecting popular changes in matters of faith and religion. Then, too, they shared a mutual sympathy for the afflicted and the downtrodden. "Blessed are the poor in spirit . . ." (Matthew 5:3) were words that appealed to Simon. Maybe he said, "With Him we can get somewhere in our just cause." Whatever the reason, Simon the Zealot was attracted to and eventually lined up with Jesus.

The story is told of a group of forty Christians who had, at Nero's order, been stripped of their clothes and driven to an ice-covered lake to freeze to death. To prevent their escape, the lake was surrounded with Roman soldiers. As they slowly stiffened with the cold, an emissary from Nero approached the group and told them that any who would recant might retire to the flaming fires which were burning at the edge of the lake. Finally, one Christian, weaker than the rest, left the band and staggered to one of the fires crying, "I give up the Christ." The Roman centurion, in command of the troops surrounding the lake, looked at him with scorn and then stripped off his armor and his underclothes and strode over to the dying band of Christians and fell to his knees in their midst, crying, "Nero could never command such devotion, I put myself under a new Commander."

Something akin to this happened to Simon the Zealot. Somewhere along the way he realized the Zealot movement would never command the loyalty and devotion men were showing to Jesus. He was awestruck by the indomitable will and magnanimous spirit of His followers so he decided to become one of them. It was a new and exciting adventure for a renegade soldier.

The greater miracle is that Jesus chose him. The very idea of inviting a vigilante, a member of a seething underground movement, a revolutionary, and a murderer to be a member of His cabinet! Why, He must have been insane. Not so. Jesus knew exactly what He was doing. He would not have extended the invitation had He questioned Simon's competence or doubted his ability to adjust to the ways of His followers. There was work for Simon to do and Jesus wisely called him to discipleship. It was another demonstration of His all-embracing love.

Have you ever watched a forest fire charge like a fiend through some wooded valley or up some hillside and then several years later, returned to the scene of that fire and noticed the cruel scars left in the wake of those hungry flames? Fire out of control is a terrible thing. By the same token, wild and unmanageable fire burning in the hearts of men is equally destructive. Hence, the necessity of holding it within the confines of usefulness. This is what Jesus did for Simon the Zealot. He held the tongues of flame that leaped like wild beasts from the caverns of his life under control. Simon still longed for the day when his people would be free from the political domination of Rome. But now his lethiferous passions were translated into a desire to build up the Kingdom of God. He was still the same zealous, flaming one, blazing with a heat which at times even put Peter to shame, but now this heat was disciplined. The flames had not been extinguished; they were simply put to work. In the words of William A. McIntyre, "There is something magnificent about the driving onrush of a personality aflame. Fierce loyalty, burning courage, blazing enthusiasm stir the most sluggish mind to admiration and often to action." The resultant transformation made Simon the Zealot a wonderfully exciting and creative person.

The years came and went and Simon lived with his Lord. He grew in mind, heart, and spirit until at last he was no longer a revolutionary fanatic, but a preacher of universal love. This is a reasonable assumption because Simon the Zealot continued as a member of Jesus' cabinet. His name appears in every list of the Twelve both before and after the Crucifixion. Furthermore, tradition says he remained a loyal and devoted servant of the church till the time of his death — preaching in Africa, in Persia, and eventually in that island country known as Great Britain.

We have ascertained within reason what kind of person Simon the Zealot was and under whose redeeming influence he fell. Might we also assume that his life story contains a message that is relevant for today? Certainly he gives us hope in the Christian life. If Jesus could ask a man of such reputation to be among His select circle of friends, there must be a place in His Kingdom for us.

Too, Simon the Zealot makes plain the mysterious power of Christlike love as illustrated in a sermon by Dr. Ed Kilbourne. During the Second World War, a nurse was at home with her family when the Nazis marched through that way. They came into the house and, in front of her, killed every member of the family. By some miracle, she was spared.

Several years later this girl was assigned to a concentration camp where she was to care for wounded soldiers. One day she came upon one of the men who had so brutally attacked and murdered the members of her family. It was a shock to see his face, but he was near death and her intrinsic love for life took charge. She nursed him. Her solicitude was imbued with kindness and love. Gradually his condition began to improve. Then one day his eyes opened. Standing beside the bed was this girl who had stayed so close during those critical hours. Presently he recognized her. "You know me?" he asked.

"Yes," came her soft reply.

"How is it then," he continued, "that you have been so good to me?"

"Because," she answered, "I am a Christian."

Something of this same forgiving spirit is evident in Simon the Zealot. Among the twelve disciples was a man named Matthew, a Jew who had sold his nation down the river for personal gain by collecting taxes from his own people and giving them to Rome. He was the kind of man Zealots hated and despised, the kind Simon would have murdered if given the chance. The interests and concerns of these two men were widely divergent and contradictory. Yet Jesus called them both to discipleship. Then, miracle of miracles! Forgiveness was effected. There were no harsh words, no fist fights, no brawls, only love and concern for the other fellow. Simon the Zealot cooperated with and labored beside one who had been his enemy. Commitment to Jesus Christ is so powerful that, when we live in the light of it, reconciliation between opposing parties is entirely possible.

Finally, Simon the Zealot calls attention to the fact that cold-hearted, lifeless, Casper Milquetoast disciples will never win the world for Jesus Christ. When the Marquis of Lansdowne became distressed about the low moral condition of the town of Colne around the turn of the last century, he wrote to the vicar to ask him what steps ought to be taken in order to improve matters. The vicar's reply was, "Send us an enthusiast." When Simon joined Jesus' band of disciples, he brought his zeal with him and it magnified the power of his witness.

There is currently a great deal of enthusiasm for those things that fracture and destroy. Repeatedly on radio, TV, and in the newspapers, we see and hear of events that disparage our unity, that renounce our oneness as Christians and as Americans. In this kind of world, apologetic, disinterested, comfortable church members will never rock a community or build the Kingdom of God. If the Word, "Jesus Christ is Lord" (Philippians 2:11), is to be heard and received we must herald that Word with the same fire and passion as those bent on destruction. A true Christian disciple is distinguished by his zeal.

11

The Inconspicuous One

It was a Thursday evening in or about A.D. 29. The scene was an upper room in the city of Jerusalem. Jesus and the members of His cabinet were seated about a table. The towel had been laid aside in anticipation of the well-known ritual of the Passover Feast. Jesus surprised the disciples by instituting a new observance. Taking the bread from the table He gave it to them saying, "This is my body which is for you" (1 Corinthians 11:24). Likewise after supper, He took the cup and gave it to them. "This cup, [He said,] is the new covenant in my blood. Do this, as often as you drink it, in remembrance of me" (1 Corinthians 11:25). It was a solemn moment. In the past, many times they had shared the fellowship of the table; together they had observed the Passover Feast. But this time it was different. Bread — body; wine — blood. What was the meaning of it all? Why the symbolism? Was it simply an experiment in the use of worship forms or was it something more? It is doubtful that any who sat about the table that night fully understood what was taking place.

Then Jesus poured out His heart. He likened the disciples

as bound to Him in God as a vine is joined to the branches (*see* John 15:5). He warned them of the persecution that awaited them (*see* John 15:18–20), and offered up the high priestly prayer which begins, "Father, the hour has come; glorify thy Son that the Son may glorify thee" (John 17:1).

Within a few hours there would follow in rapid succession Gethsemane, the arrest, the trials, the Crucifixion, and death. All that Jesus had said and done was to prepare the disciples for this separation, to strengthen them for this ordeal.

Now He tried to comfort the disciples. He said, "Let not your hearts be troubled; believe in God; believe also in me. In my Father's house are many rooms; if it were not so, would I have told you that I go to prepare a place for you?" (John 14:1, 2). Then He offered the wonderful promise: "I will not leave you desolate; I will come to you. Yet a little while, and the world will see me no more, but you will see me" (John 14:18, 19).

At this point one of the disciples interrupted Him. Judas, not Iscariot, asked, "Lord, how is it that you will manifest yourself to us, and not to the world?" (John 14:22). We know very little about the man who asked this question. Aside from his name appearing in the lists of the Twelve and this one incident, the New Testament tells nothing about him. However, by piecing together the fragments of information which can be gleaned from the Scriptures and from tradition, we can make some inferences that will give a reasonable judgment about his character.

Judas (not Iscariot), or Thaddaeus as he was more often called, was a follower, not a leader. Had he been a more prominent member of Jesus' cabinet, a vital force in the development and expansion of the early Christian community, we would have heard more about him. He remained silent, inconspicuous, and unknown.

Nevertheless, this disciple was a *big* man. By this I mean in heart, in disposition, and in spirit. We can honestly say this for at least four reasons. First, because of his name. Ordinarily a name is simply a ready means of distinguishing one person from another, a tag we put on each other for the convenience of the postman. But such has not always been the case. In the Bible particularly, names are frequently used not just to distinguish a man from his neighbor, but to reveal some pertinent information about his character or his career. Accordingly, *Jacob*, which means supplanter, was renamed *Israel*, which means striver-with-God, to indicate that he has striven with God and men and won. Joseph was told in a dream that Mary would bear him a Son and that His name should be called Jesus because He would save His people from their sins (*see* Matthew 1:21), and *Jesus*, properly interpreted, means God is Salvation. When Andrew brought his brother to Christ, the Lord said, "Thou art Simon the son of Jona." But under the influence of Christ, Simon became a new person. So Jesus changed his name: "Thou shalt be called Cephas, which is by interpretation, A stone" (John 1:42 KJV), something strong and unshakable. In the Bible at least, to know a man's name was in many instances to know the man himself.

Such exactly might have been the case here. This disciple's original name was Judas Lebbaeus, but evidently the disciples preferred the nickname Thaddaeus. Thus, his full name came to be Judas Thaddaeus Lebbaeus. When Judas is used, the gospel writers are always careful to add the words *Not Iscariot* to distinguish him from the betrayer.

Notice that *Thaddaeus* when interpreted from the Aramaic means the bold or the courageous one. The inference being that he was not afraid of danger, that he would stand tall in the face of adversity or conflict, that he would give his life, if need be, in order to save the life of another.

Note, too, that *Lebbaeus* when interpreted from the Aramaic means the hearty one. The inference here being Thaddaeus was good company—warm, friendly, affable. He was a robust extrovert, the kind of man who enjoyed living his life to the hilt. Today he would make a good salesman, an effective personnel administrator, or an entertaining toastmaster.

Silent, inconspicuous, unknown! Yes, this was Thaddaeus. But, if his name holds a clue to his character, we can assume that he was bold and courageous, a man of strong and sturdy convictions, warm and affectionate in all of his human relationships.

Secondly, we can believe Thaddaeus was a *big* man because Jesus selected him as one of the Twelve. I cannot imagine a president of the United States reaching down into the grass-roots of America and pulling to Washington as a member of his cabinet a man who has no leadership ability, who has low moral standards, who is prone to the making of mistakes, who is stubborn and unwilling to learn. Why, to give such a man the ranking status of a cabinet member would be disastrous, not only to the administration, but to the federal government and our nation as a whole. By the same token, I cannot imagine Jesus choosing as a close and most trusted friend anyone whom He believed to be unworthy of the position. The disciples were unlearned and ill-prepared to fulfill the responsibilities of their office. This is an accepted fact, but they were big in spirit, with infinite capacity for love and learning and labor. Thaddaeus must have been of this caliber, else our Lord would have passed him by in favor of someone else.

Thirdly, we can believe Thaddaeus was a *big* man because of his questioning disposition. One of the principal differences between the big person and the little person is the use they make of interrogation. The small fry is more given to talking than to listening. He has much to say, but there is little which he cares to know. The big man has the questioning habit. He is always trying to learn. If by his silence, we can assume Thaddaeus spent his time with Jesus watching, listening, and observing, then we can believe he was this kind of man. When something was said which he did not understand, Thaddaeus had the courage to ask for clarification: "Lord," he said, "I'm puzzled. How can Your Kingdom be kept secret when You have already broadcast its coming from the housetops?" (*see* John 14:22). It was an intelligent question honestly, openly, and passionately presented. Evidently Jesus thought so by the pains He took in answering it. Being able to ask the right question is a far better sign of character than thinking you know all the right answers.

Finally, we can believe Thaddaeus was a *big* man because he was not given to the making of snap judgments. Jesus answered him by saying, "The secrets of My Kingdom are to be whispered into the ears of those who love and obey Me. But anyone in the world is free to love and obey" (*see* John 14:23). Thaddaeus did not understand. He could not grasp the trenchant meaning of the statement, but he stayed around to see what was going to happen before making his final decision.

Pontius Pilate also asked Jesus a vital question. "What is truth?" (John 18:38). But Pilate was nervous and fidgety, so afraid of what Jesus' answer was going to be that he quickly hurried on to another matter. Not so Thaddaeus. He listened intently and then stayed with the disciples to see if what had been said was true. Sure enough, he discovered that Jesus could be seen only through the eyes of faith, that He could be known only by those who loved Him. After the Resurrection, Jesus did not confront Caiaphas and say, "Well, here I am alive again, hale and hearty, ready to drive more money changers out of the temple!" He did not walk into Pilate's judgment hall to say, "Pilate, you failed. You thought you had killed Me, but you didn't. I'm starting tomorrow on a larger preaching mission!" No, to Pilate and Caiaphas, and all the unbelieving multitude, Jesus was dead and remained dead.

Only those whose souls were attuned to His recognized Him in the Upper Room (*see* Acts 1:13), on the Emmaus Road (*see* Luke 24:13–35), beside the sea (*see* John 21:4–14), and on the crest of Olivet (*see* Acts 1:6–12). That Thaddaeus was a part of this ecstatic and intoxicating experience suggests that he was not prone to arrive at conclusions hastily or to the making of snap judgments.

This disciple was a follower, not a leader. He was big in heart, in disposition, and in spirit. He was also a loyal and devoted servant of Jesus Christ. We know this because his name appears among the Twelve after Pentecost. We know this, too, because of stories about his work and witness in the church which have been handed down through ancient tradition. One of the most beautiful of these is recorded by Eusebius in his *The Ecclesiastical History*. It identifies Thaddaeus with the healing of Abgar, king of Edessa, who was stricken with leprosy.

Having heard of Jesus' miracles, Abgar sent a letter in which he asked Jesus to come and cure his disease. He offered Him a share of his kingdom so that He might escape the malice of the Jerusalem Jews. Jesus declined the invitation because He felt there was still work to be done where He was, but He promised Abgar that after His Ascension He would send one of His disciples. Sure enough, after the Ascension Thaddaeus arrived in Edessa, healed Abgar, and converted the whole community.

Tradition also states that Thaddaeus preached in Persia and Armenia and that he died in agonizing torture from the wounds of arrows. He was truly a dynamic disciple, a loyal and devoted servant of Jesus Christ.

12

The Disciple From Missouri

You may think it too modern to call Thomas the Disciple From Missouri. Yet the description is an apt one. He had to be shown before he would believe.

> Seeing is believing
> Was his motto. Better,
> Feeling is believing.
> The scientific mind requires
> Substantial evidence,
> Controlled experiments,
> With photographs and measurements.
> And Thomas was no poet,
> Nor would he credit women —
> Or even ten apostles.
> He required the touch
> Of his ten fingers.
>
> EUTYCHAS

In Copenhagen's Thorwaldsen Museum, he is depicted in stone with a finger to his mouth, as though in serious contemplation, and a carpenter's square under his arm. Since we are living in a practical, scientific, show-me world, Thomas is a member of Jesus' cabinet with whom we should feel very much at home.

The Synoptic Gospels tell nothing about him other than his name. It is in the fourth gospel that his personality comes to life. *Thomas* is the Aramaic word for twin or the Greek *Didymus*, which has given rise to some interesting speculations: that he had a twin sister, Lydia; that he was the twin of another disciple; that he was the twin brother of Jesus. We simply do not know who was his twin. Because Thomas was among the seven disciples who, following the Crucifixion, returned to the Sea of Galilee, some believe he was a fisherman. But tradition states that by trade he was a carpenter and a stone mason. In either case, we can assume he was a strong, robust, muscular and hardheaded man. Certainly he was a dynamic disciple, the kind of person with whom modern man can discover a veritable affinity. We readily identify with Thomas because he was prone to view the dark side of things, to be pessimistic in his attitude and approach to life.

On the television program, "Mayberry R.F.D.," Goober was having difficulty with a new division manager who pressured him into modernizing his service station operation. An up-to-date sales program was launched, but the new approach did not fit either Mayberry or Goober. Goober was so unhappy he decided to go out of business. Almost immediately Howard Spragg, one of the fine citizens of Mayberry, began to prophesy the doom of their community. He saw the closing of the filling station as a sign of bad times. This was Thomas. He had a tendency to see the extreme difficulty in every situation.

One of Jesus' very dear friends, Lazarus, whose home had been a favorite place for rest and refreshment, was critically ill and the family had asked for Him. A few days previously

Jesus had barely escaped from the vicinity of Jerusalem with His life. Naturally the disciples protested His return to Bethany. The risk was too great, the danger too real. "Rabbi, the Jews were but now seeking to stone you, [they said,] and are you going there again?" (John 11:8). Jesus did wait two days before making a decision. Then He said, "Lazarus is dead; and for your sakes I am glad that I was not there, so that you may believe. But let us go to him" (John 11:14, 15). He was going to Bethany despite their counsel. The disciples were upset by such reckless abandon and were in the mood to desert Him when the normally silent Thomas exclaimed, "Let us also go, that we may die with him" (John 11:16). He would go with his Lord, but his pessimism would permit him to see only the trouble that awaited them. You might say he walked on the shady rather than the sunny side of the street.

We identify with Thomas because he is known for his faults. Shakespeare, in *Julius Caesar*, said,

> The evil men do lives after them,
> The good is oft interred with their bones.

Sports fans remember Wrong Way Riegels, the football player on the West Coast who, during the 1929 Rose Bowl game, became confused and ran the wrong way with the ball setting up a touchdown for his opponents. It was a terrible mistake, one Riegels has never been able to live down despite the fact that on hundreds of other occasions he ran the right way, and ran exceptionally well. We remember the blue note of the concert pianist and forget the dozens of musical scores played without a flaw. Our nature is to overlook the good and cling to the evil.

Thomas was a good man—one of the most loyal, devoted, and conscientious members of Jesus' cabinet. He left his home, family, friends, and job to become a disciple. He listened attentively to the pearls of wisdom that fell from the lips of his Master. On at least one occasion he went with Jesus to Jerusalem despite his fear of almost certain death. But he could not believe the Easter miracle. "Unless I see in his hands the print of the nails, and place my finger in the mark of the nails, and place my hand in his side, I will not believe" (John 20:25). One doubt in the midst of countless expressions of belief and history has saddled him with the ignominious epithet, The Doubting Disciple. It is one of those apparent cruelties we are forever inflicting upon our fellow men. Thomas is known not for the certitude to which he eventually came, but for his faults; not for the good things he did, but for his one mistake.

We identify with Thomas because in the crucible of sorrow he wanted to be alone. Walking through the valley of the shadow of death is never easy. In it people often ask, "Why do I dread to go to church?" So here. Jesus was crucified, dead, and buried. For Thomas it was the end; it was as if the whole world had caved in. All hope for the establishment of the Kingdom of God died with his Lord. The tragedy did something to him. He did not want to talk with anyone, even his closest friends. He just ducked his head and crawled like a wounded animal to some solitary place to lick his wounds and ponder the future. No wonder Thomas was not present in the Upper Room when Jesus appeared to the disciples! To have sought comfort in the solitude of his own spirit was a perfectly natural thing for him to have done.

We identify with Thomas because he experienced the pangs of regret. When the report of Jesus' Resurrection was given to him, Thomas could not believe it. He was skeptical and doubting. He thought his brethren had had an hallucination. At this point, he would have agreed with Renon, the French

writer who said, "The disciples were not deceivers but vision-
aries led astray by an emotional woman, Mary Magdalene."
Still, the disciples were different men. Their doubts had given
way to certainty, their sense of defeat to a consciousness of
victory, their despair to joy. The transformation was obvious.
In the days following, Thomas must have thought a thousand
times, "If only I had been there. If only I had seen Him
perhaps I, too, would have believed." It was not that God had
forsaken him; he had forsaken God. Making this discovery, the
Disciple From Missouri lamented his absence.

We identify with Thomas because he struggled with the
problems of faith and belief. Pascal wrote, "There are two
classes of men who can be called reasonable, those who serve
God with all their heart because they know Him, or those who
seek for Him with their whole heart because they know Him
not. I have nothing but compassion for all who sincerely
lament their doubt, who look upon it as the worst of evils, and
spare no pains to escape from it. . . ." This was Thomas. His
doubt was not the hardened unbelief of the Pharisees, nor evidence of positive indifference. It was an honest quest for
truth. He struggled to believe.

In the Lazarus incident, he showed a loyalty to Jesus despite
the fear of almost certain death. Granted it was a shallow
commitment, a "two-o'clock-in-the-morning courage," but
Thomas *did* go with his Lord to Bethany. It was a significant
step forward in his quest for faith.

On the occasion of the Passover Feast in the Upper Room,
Jesus prepared the disciples for the events that were to follow.
"Let not your hearts be troubled; [He said,] believe in God,
believe also in me. In my Father's house are many rooms; if it
were not so, would I have told you that I go to prepare a place
for you? And when I go and prepare a place for you, I will
come again and will take you to myself, that where I am you

may be also. And you know the way where I am going" (John 14:1–4).

Thomas did not understand. His practical mind demanded a road map, something he could see. "Lord, [he asked,] we do not know where you are going; how can we know the way?" (John 14:5).

Jesus replied, "I am the way, and the truth and the life" (John 14:6). It was as though He had said, "Thomas, what you need is not an argument but a presence, and I am offering you Myself." Thomas did not really comprehend the implications of the statement. Nevertheless, that he asked a question which provoked such a response is in itself evidence of his constant struggle to believe.

Then followed Gethsemane, the trial, the Crucifixion, and the Resurrection. When news of this extraordinary event reached Thomas, he was reluctant to believe. We have every right to assume the announcement caused him much mental anguish, that it made him wrestle with his doubts as he had never done before.

Eight days later, Jesus appeared again to the disciples. This time Thomas was among them. Jesus approached him and said, "Put your finger here, and see my hands; and put out your hand, and place it in my side; do not be faithless but believing" (John 20:27). There is no indication that the Disciple From Missouri accepted the offer. He simply fell to his knees and exclaimed, "My Lord and my God!" (John 20:28). Seeing was enough. His belief had become real at last.

The late Dr. Roy L. Smith tells of an unusual fear of the dark he had as a boy. One night his father asked him to go to the barn for some tools. He confessed to his father that he was afraid of the dark. The father put a lantern in his hand. "How far can you see, son?"

"As far as the mulberry tree," he said.

"Then go out to the mulberry tree." When the boy arrived there his father asked, "Now how far can you see."

"I can see to the currant bushes."

When the boy arrived at the currant bushes his father asked, "How far can you see from there?" This time it was the henhouse. Next it was the hog lot, and finally the barn. And so the boy, step by step, made it to the barn.

It was the same with Thomas. He could not see the end from the beginning. There was much about the darkness that was frightening, but Jesus provided him with a lantern. He courageously walked in the light the lantern provided. It was a slow and painful journey, an uphill climb all the way, a tremendous battle, but in the end faith won. Thomas moved at last from disbelief to belief, from uncertainty to certainty, from doubt to dedication.

We can identify with the Disciple From Missouri. We can also learn a great deal from him. His life story is a series of object lessons in how to achieve faith. He teaches the value of an open and inquiring mind. Thomas did not wait until all of his questions were answered before becoming a member of Jesus' cabinet.

Recently I had occasion to visit with a man who for years has wanted to make a public profession of his faith in Jesus Christ and to take the vows of church membership, but he has consistently postponed the making of this decision because he feels incapable of living up to it. Thomas was not of this nature. Oh, he doubted. He was skeptical. He wanted to be absolutely sure, to be shown before he believed, but he did not sit around and wait for all of his difficulties to be straightened out before accepting the responsibilities of discipleship. When Jesus called, he responded.

Thomas did not give up when the going was rough. This is

one of the reasons why so many marriages wind up in the divorce court. Couples standing before the altar of the church are inclined to view each other and their life together through rose-colored glasses. They are in love, but one day soon thereafter the honeymoon ends. When these couples wake to the realization that marriage demands the involvement of their whole being, the working out of life's nitty-gritty problems in some amicable fashion, sometimes they are overwhelmed by it. When this happens, deterioration sets in. Unless something is done to stop it the end result will be disastrous, possibly the divorce court. Thomas was not this kind of person. Granted, he was slow to believe, but he was not one to give up, to turn back, to shrink from unpleasant consequences.

When it became obvious that Jesus was going to Bethany, despite their counsel, he said to the other disciples, "Let us also go, that we may die with him" (John 11:16). As a boy who could not swim, Thomas stood on the bank shivering and shaking—afraid to take the plunge, but somehow by God's grace he did. He found enough courage to become involved, to go out on a limb with his Lord, and, if necessary, to die with Him. "Forward March"—in good times or bad, doubts or no doubts—was his approach to discipleship.

Thomas was in no great hurry to believe. Most people are like the four-year-old boy in the Sunday school. The teacher was preparing the class for Easter. She held a cocoon in her hand and said, "Children, this is a cocoon. In it a big worm is asleep. He has been sleeping a long time. But soon he will wake up and come out of his shell as a beautiful butterfly."

The child interrupted: "Where is the butterfly now?"

The teacher tried as best she could to explain and promised, "If you will wait a few weeks, I'll show you the butterfly."

But don't you know—a few days later the cocoon was found

broken open and the lifeless worm exposed to the cold air. The little boy could not wait. He had to see the answer right now. In so doing, he destroyed the beauty that faith in time's disclosure could have revealed.

I have often wondered what might have happened to Judas Iscariot had he postponed that final act of self-destruction just a few more hours, had he only doubted his doubts a little longer. The outcome of his life would have been altered considerably, but he could not wait.

Thomas demonstrated greater wisdom. He could not accept the Easter miracle. "Unless I see in his hands the print of the nails, and place my finger in the mark of the nails, and place my hand in his side, I will not believe" (John 20:25). But observe; he did not desert the ship. He did not leave the community of faith. He did not run away or wallow in self-pity. For eight long and miserable days, Thomas waited (and I am convinced that had it been necessary he would have waited still longer) before he was able to affirm his faith in Jesus Christ. Maybe if we struggled with our unbelief a little longer, dug a little deeper for the nuggets of truth, we, too, would be able to say with conviction, "My Lord and my God!" (John 20:28).

Thomas was perfectly amenable to change. He wanted so desperately to believe that he was willing to be shown or convinced. There are many stubborn people in the world. Once persuaded of the rightness of an idea, they cling to that idea even though it may have been proved false. I think particularly of the Flat Earth Society. However, since the successful Apollo flights to the moon, the members of this group have begun to admit some misgivings about their basic philosophy. It takes a great deal of courage for a man to swallow his doubts, to take back his questions, to admit that he was wrong. Thomas was this kind of person. He was open and receptive to new ideas and fresh insights.

We can identify with the Disciple From Missouri; we can learn from him; and finally, we can honorably pattern our lives after him. To emulate Thomas would be to discover life at its best. He was bold and courageous.

A little boy one day overheard some of his playmates talk about sleeping out in a tent. He was interested. Later, he shared this interest with his father. "Well, son," he said, "if you would like me to, I'll borrow a tent and sleep out in the yard with you some night."

The little fellow thought about the matter for several days and then went to his mother about it. "I've decided," he said, "I do want to sleep in a tent. Will you make me one?"

"Where do you want it?" she inquired.

"Oh," he promptly answered, "up in my room right beside my bed!"

The small boy desperately wanted to do the bold and adventuresome thing, but somehow he lacked the courage to break away from familiar surroundings. Not so Thomas. When Jesus called him to discipleship, he immediately responded even though he knew it meant being uprooted from his past. It takes a brave man to leave the warmth and security of the commonplace and well-known and move out into a sphere of life that is strangely new and different. Yet Thomas was so interested in the work and witness of Jesus Christ that he was perfectly willing to take this risk, and did!

This same courage was demonstrated in the Upper Room when Thomas inquired of his Lord: "We do not know where you are going; how can we know the way?" (John 14:5). Generally, men take great pride in their ability to comprehend or to grasp the meaning of an idea. Knowing this, we can better appreciate how difficult, how hard it was for Thomas to admit in a public gathering that he did not understand.

We see it, too, in his ultimate declaration of faith, "My Lord and my God!" (John 20:28) When Jesus did at last reveal Himself, Thomas was quick to pull down his flag of stubborn unbelief. Some have said that it was always Thomas's first reaction not to do what he was told to do and not to believe what he was asked to believe. In a sense this is true. Thomas was slow to act, but behind this facade was a bold and courageous spirit whose example lifts a soul like music to the light.

He was wise in his choice of companions. Thomas could have gone to school at the synagogue where he might have studied under some of the most learned men of his day, enjoyed the finest physical facilities, had access to the very best library resources, had the assurance of three square meals a day, and a comfortable place to sleep every night. But no! He would not be taken in by external appearances nor be tempted by the authoritative credentials of the priests who taught there. Thomas was looking for challenge, for character, for commitment, and for creativity, so he gave himself to a young upstart itinerate Preacher from the little village of Nazareth. It was a wise decision.

Have you ever noticed that during their association Jesus never scolded Thomas for his doubts? He knew that doubt is the father of discovery, that a questioning spirit is perfectly normal and necessary in the development of a growing person.

> There lives more faith in honest doubt,
> Believe me, than in half the creeds.
>   ALFRED LORD TENNYSON

Jesus respected Thomas's honest quest for truth. He also recognized a quality of love we often overlook. When confronted with Thomas's doubt, Jesus did not panic. He did not rush right in as most of us would have done and provide him

with an immediate answer. On the contrary, He deliberately
let Thomas stew for a while in his own misery. He waited
eight days before revealing Himself to this dynamic disciple.
It was not a condemnation, but a way of meeting unbelief
with sympathy and understanding. Jesus knew well what the
Apostle Paul later put in words, "Love is patient. . ." (1 Corinthians 13:4).

The School of Christ may not have been able to offer him a
degree in higher education, provide him with a plush office in
which to work, or assure him of financial security, but its Dean
was a great Man and Teacher.

Then, too, Thomas could have chosen his friends from the
Pharisees whom everyone admired, from the members of the
local carpenter's union to which he belonged, or from the
crowd that mingled for their daily gossip sessions in the
village square. Instead, he chose his friends from among the
followers of Jesus Christ. Again it was a very wise choice.

Never did one of the disciples say, "Thomas, you're through
here. Out you go. You can't stay in our midst because you are
a heretic, a skeptic, and an unbeliever." No one ever said,
"Thomas, you can't speak on the campus of our church college
lest you wreck the dynamic faith of our students there." The
disciples loved him not because of his unbelief, but for his
struggle to believe. They genuinely helped him achieve it.
Dr. Earl Marlatt often told his students at Perkins School of
Theology, "You are not all of yourself, your friends are the
rest of you." Thomas made a wise choice of companions.

He saw the necessity of total commitment to Jesus Christ.
Once convinced of the truth, Thomas acted upon it without
reservation. Consequently, his remaining years were spent in
devoted service to others and in building the Kingdom of God.
Harry Emerson Fosdick in his autobiography, *The Living of
These Days*, tells of the doubts that beset him in his sophomore
year at college. He writes, "Wild horses could not have

dragged me to church." Then he began to doubt his doubts, to fight against the darkness, emerging finally with a radiant faith which for half a century he freely shared with millions of people throughout the world.

A friend tells of a troubled black minister who sought an interview with Fosdick when he was an active pastor at Riverside Church, New York. His datebook was filled, but Fosdick felt he must help the brokenhearted minister. The interview lasted for two hours, and when the black minister emerged, his face aglow with new hope, he said, "What a wonderful man! When I entered that room a while ago, every star in my sky had fallen. Now he has put every one of them back in place again." Because Fosdick had to fight to keep the stars of faith and hope in his own sky, he was able, under God, to put them back into the skies of other people.

This was the case with Thomas. Since he arrived at his belief through the "dark night of the soul" he was able to minister more effectively to others. His life story illustrates the thought that those who pass through the valley of doubt usually emerge with a stronger faith than those who never doubted at all. As Robert Browning says in *The Transformation of the Twelve*, "The more of doubt, the stronger faith, I say, If faith o'ercomes doubt."

Thomas's later years are clothed in mystery, but tradition claims that he carried that good news of the Resurrection experience to India where the congregation of Saint Thomas claims him as their founder. No other member of Jesus' original cabinet has a church which he founded still active. Rumor also has it that he was martyred in Madros by a lance thrust into his side.

Identify with this young and dynamic disciple. Let him teach you how to achieve faith. Emulate his courage, his wisdom in choosing companions, and his commitment to Jesus Christ. This is life at its best.

III

The Epilogue

A glorious band, the chosen few
On whom the Spirit came,
Twelve valiant saints, their hope they knew,
And mocked the cross and flame;
.   .   .   .

They climbed the steep ascent of heaven
Through peril, toil, and pain.
O God, to us may grace be given
To follow in their train.

REGINALD HEBUR

Discipleship in Today's World

Every great leader of men has made clear the terms of his discipleship. Following the siege of Rome in 1849, the Italian patriot Garibaldi voiced a stirring challenge to his soldiers: "Soldiers, what I have to offer you is fatigue, danger, struggle and death; the chill of the cold night in the free air, and heat under the burning sun; no lodgings, no munitions, no provisions, but forced marches, dangerous watch posts, and continual struggle with bayonets against batteries. Those who love freedom and their country may follow me."

In the dark days of the Second World War, when Sir Winston Churchill took over the helm of the floundering British ship of state, he promised his people not a bed of roses, but blood, sweat, toil, and tears.

King Arthur, whose nobility has been held in highest esteem by all English-speaking people,

Bound them [his knights] by so straight vows to his own self,
That when they rose, knighted from kneeling, some
Were pale as at the passing of a ghost,

119

Some flush'd, and others dazed, as one who wakes
Half-blinded at the coming of a light.

ALFRED LORD TENNYSON

But no other leader required such straight vows as Jesus. He never hid the sharp demand or compromised with principle. To the enthusiasts who approached Him with the thought of becoming disciples, He said, "Have you sat down to count the cost?" (*See* Luke 14:28.)

To James and John who sought preferment in the Kingdom of God, He said, "Are you willing to drink My cup of suffering?" (*See* Matthew 20:20–22.)

To the rich young ruler who longed for a more satisfying life, He said, "Can you place your love for people ahead of your love for things?" (*See* Matthew 19:16–22.)

Jesus did not come into the world to make life easy, but to make men great. His commands were consistently clear and decisive; His demands daring and difficult. "If any man would come after me, let him deny himself and take up his cross and follow me" (Mark 8:34).

The remarkable thing is men responded. Generally they were poor, rough, and unlearned. But they were so arrested by His presence, so enthralled by His message, so encouraged by His optimism and hopefulness, they forsook all to follow Him. By means of this commitment, the disciples became recipients of unbelievable power. They changed lives, gave birth to the church, and significantly altered the course of history. No wonder we speak of them as dynamic disciples!

But how about us? Is there a place for modern man in Jesus' circle of friends? If so, what are the conditions of Christian discipleship in today's world? First, there must be a profession of our faith. We have to make up our minds to accept Jesus Christ as Lord and Savior.

Several years ago a plane crashed on the runway at Philadelphia and caught fire. At the door, the attractive twenty-four-year-old stewardess Mary Frances Housley took her place to help the passengers to the ground. Just as she was ready to jump, a woman on the ground screamed, "My baby, my baby!" Frankie Housley then turned into the plane to find the woman's baby. That was the last time anyone saw her alive. When the debris had cooled, they found Mary Frances's body over the four-month-old baby she had tried to rescue. When *Time* magazine ran the story, the caption under her picture read, "She could have jumped." Life demands decision. We do not have to risk our lives for the gospel any more than Mary Frances Housley had to go back into that burning plane. Notice how Jesus said, "If any man would come after me. . . ." It was His way of saying, "You don't have to follow Me. No one is going to force you into My circle of friends."

> Once to every man and nation
> Comes the moment to decide,
> In the strife of truth with falsehood,
> For the good or evil side.
>   JAMES RUSSELL LOWELL

Discipleship begins when we are able to say and mean it, "I want to be one of Christ's men, I want to walk in the light of His love."

A second condition of Christian discipleship in today's world is self-denial. We must make a profession of our faith in Jesus Christ. Then we must pursue that faith with a divine passion. Ordinarily, we think of self-denial as the giving up of something, but it is really a friendly and helpful discipline. It is a way of cultivating a taste for those things that will last and of making life's choices on the basis of what is most creative.

After all, there are just two forms of sacrifice: we can deny ourselves the worst for the best or we can deny ourselves the best for the worst. In either case we pay. A man who chooses to be a philanderer throws away all restraints, stops at nothing to satisfy his passions. The word *discipline* is foreign to his way of living. But, while he refuses to deny himself the fleeting enjoyment of sensual pleasures, he does deny himself the chance of a happy home, and the respect of a good woman. He never appreciates such enduring values as love, loyalty, and lasting friendship. Saying "yes" to one way of life automatically means saying "no" to another.

Up to the age of twenty, William Lyon Phelps heartily disliked classical music. He enjoyed brass bands and comic operas, but classical music was something he attempted to evade. However, under the pressure of a friend's urging, he finally went to hear a very fine orchestra in New Haven. The program that night was Beethoven and Wagner. "Never shall I forget," he writes, "the boredom of that evening, I really suffered. It was genuine agony and distress. I gazed idly over the audience to see how my fellow sufferers were enduring it. Some of them were asleep. How I envied them! The hideous noises were going ahead on the stage, but those blissful souls were free from pain." He came to the conclusion, however, that his failure to appreciate classical music might be his fault. At any rate, he decided to hear it again. The second time he found that it wasn't quite so boring. He kept on going. With his increasing interest in attendance, this music of a higher order began to appeal to him. "And today," he said, "I would rather hear a competent orchestra play Beethoven and Wagner than hear anything else in the world."

In the same fashion, we can discover that the finer and cleaner things of mind and heart and speech are really more palatable. By denying ourselves the worst in favor of the best we can acquire a taste for those things that have lasting value.

Self-denial is a positive way of training for the religious life.

A third condition for discipleship is performance. We must profess our faith in Jesus Christ. We must pursue that faith with a relentless courage. Then, we must relate that faith to life. We must give it practical demonstration and this sometimes necessitates the carrying of a cross.

A black boy in California was putting himself through college by working in a service station. Some of the people in the community, however, objected to being served by a black. They threatened to take their business some place else if the employer did not do something about it. So the employer, not wanting to lose any of his customers, decided that the only thing he could do was let the young man go.

There were some in the community who thought, "Isn't it unfortunate. Somebody ought to do something about it." One lady, who was in no way responsible for the situation, did something about it. She approached the boy's employer and asked, "How many customers do you think you will lose if you keep this young man?"

"Oh, I suppose possibly eighteen or twenty," he said.

She then replied: "If I get you twenty new customers, will you keep him?"

He answered, "I guess I would."

She did even better. She got him twenty-five new customers. This, despite the counsel of friends who repeatedly told her she had no business getting mixed up in the matter.

For years, I have longed to see the famous Passion Play at Oberammergau, Germany. The story is told of some American tourists who were visiting with the actor playing the part of Christ. He was getting ready to do the scene in which the Via Dolorosa to Calvary is portrayed. A woman turned to her husband and said, "Why don't we take a picture of you with the cross?" They politely asked if it would be all right.

When the actor assented to their request, the man bent

down to lift the cross on his back. But it was too heavy. "Why, in heaven's name, do you make it so heavy?" he asked. "One made of papier-mâché would look as well."

The actor replied: "Sir, I could not play the part of Christ if I did not feel the weight of His cross."

Neither can we. As a berry bush is valued not by the fewness of its thorns but by the quantity and quality of its fruit, so a disciple of Jesus Christ is measured not by loose talk and public commitment but by the quantity and quality of his performance. "So with faith; if it does not lead to action, it is in itself a lifeless thing" (James 2:17 NEB).

The final condition of discipleship in today's world is perseverance. We are called not to watch or to imitate Jesus but to follow Him. This entails far more than a single decision; it requires daily renewal of our loyalty and dedication. After the Duke of Wellington had defeated Napoleon at the Battle of Waterloo, he remarked that it was accomplished not because the British soldiers were braver than the French soldiers but simply because they were brave five minutes longer. A true disciple of Jesus Christ is one who carries on for Him five minutes longer. He follows through.

The Reverend Donald B. Strobe relates this personal experience: "When I was a layman, a minister came to ask if my wife and I would serve as counselors for a youth group. I told him that it was funny that just that day we had decided that we were so grateful to God for His blessings that we would never say 'no' to the church again. The minister said: 'That's a pretty dangerous thing to do.' It is. It led me from counseling to college to seminary, and here I am a minister."

When you hear God calling and follow through on that call, you never know where you'll end. That's part of the excitement of the Christian life. It is like falling in love and getting married. When a couple stand before an altar and take the wedding vows, neither knows what lies ahead, but they love each other and are willing to risk the future in each other's hands. They are willing to take what comes because they know they will cope with it together.

So life with Jesus. It gets richer and finer as the years come and go, provided, of course, we are constant in our commitment. A Christian disciple keeps on keeping on for his Lord.

An Australian author, Miss Manning, had loved and been loved in return. Her lover was going to India and wished to bare his heart. He wrote her and asked her not to reply if she could not let him hope. If she sent no answer, he would take her silence not as giving consent, but denial. Miss Manning found no fault with this letter, but wrote her reply and sent it within the hour. It was a pouring wet day and her brother undertook to take the letter to the village post office. Her lover never came. Some years later she heard of his marriage and of his remaining in India, where he had an honorable and prosperous career. Twenty-five years later, the Manning family moved into a new house and an old coat belonging to the brother was brought into the light. When the pockets were turned out, there the letter was, yellow and crumpled, but with the seal unbroken and the stamp untouched. The culprit was never told and the lost lover never knew.

Now we have been entrusted with God's great love letter to the world. The members of Jesus' cabinet were faithful in delivering that letter. Will we be equally as faithful?

Bibliography

Applegarth, Margaret T. *Right Here, Right Now.* New York: Harper & Brothers, 1950.

Arlon, Laura. "The Extra Hand." *Accent on Youth* 1(1969).

Barclay, William. *The Master's Men.* Nashville: Abingdon Press, 1959.

Barker, William P. *Twelve Who Were Chosen.* Old Tappan: Fleming H. Revell Company, 1957.

Burns, John W. "Judas: The Confused Confession." *The Sermon Golden* 14(1967)8.

Chappell, Clovis. *Faces About the Cross.* Nashville: Abingdon Press, 1951.

Croschatt, Frank Q. "Transforming Companionship." *The Sermon Builder* (1962)16.

Edwards, Tyson; Catrevas, C. N.; Edwards, Johnathan; and Brown, Ralph Emerson. *The New Dictionary of Thoughts.* Bloomington: Standard Book Co., 1959.

Eutychas. "Thomas." *Christianity Today* 4(1965)18.

Ferm, Vergilius. *An Encyclopedia of Religion.* New York: The Philosophical Library, 1945.

Ferris, Frank Halliday. "Jesus and the Ordinary People." *Pulpit Digest* 7–8(1961)56.

Foote, Gaston. *Footnotes.* Old Tappan: Fleming H. Revell Company, 1956.

Foote, Gaston. *How God Helps*. Nashville: Abingdon Press, 1966.

Foote, Gaston. *The Transformation of the Twelve*. Nashville: Abingdon Press, 1958.

Gibbons, Nancy. "The Quiet People." *Guideposts* 2(1966)27.

Goer, Joseph. *The Lore of the New Testament*. Boston: Little, Brown & Co., 1952.

Goodrich, Robert E., Jr. "Weep for Yourselves." Sermon preached on "The Protestant Hour," 12(1965)4.

Harris, Frank Halliday. "Let Your Light Shine." *Pulpit Digest* 2(1967)39.

Kennedy, Gerald. "The Starting Line." *Pulpit Digest* 4(1969)59.

Kohn, Harold E. *Thoughts Afield, Meditations Through the Seasons*. Grand Rapids: Wm. B. Eerdmans Publishing Co., 1959, 1961.

Kraeling, Emil G. *The Disciples*. Chicago: Rand McNally & Co., 1966.

Ledbetter, E. L. Article. *Survey* vol.3 no.16(1961)17.

Lindquist, Raymond Irving. *Notes for Living*. Philadelphia: J. P. Lippincott Co., 1968.

Marshall, Catherine. *Mr. Jones, Meet the Master*. Old Tappan: Fleming H. Revell Company, 1950.

McIntyre, William A. *Christ's Cabinet*. New York: The Salvation Army, Inc., 1937.

Nelson, C. Ellis. "Choosing a God." *The Pulpit* 9(1960)23.

Nelson, David A. "The Disciple from Missouri." Sermon preached at Highland Baptist Church, 12 July 1959, at Louisville, Kentucky. Mimeographed.

Nelson, David A. "Unknown, Yet Well Known." Sermon preached at Highland Baptist Church, 19 July 1959, at Louisville, Kentucky. Mimeographed.

Norton, William. "Truth Illuminated." *The New Sermon Builder* vol.16 no.7(1960)19.

Quillian, Paul. *Not a Sparrow Falls*. Nashville: Abingdon Press, 1952.

Redhead, John A. *Sermons on Bible Characters*. Nashville: Abingdon Press, 1963.

Reid, John Calvin. *We Knew Jesus.* Grand Rapids: Wm. B. Eerdmans Publishing Co., 1954.

Rice, Helen Steiner. *Just for You, a Collection of Inspirational Verses.* Cincinnati: Gibson Greeting Cards, Inc., 1963.

Sangster, W. E. *They Met at Calvary.* Nashville: Abingdon Press, 1956.

Shamblin, J. Kenneth. *Life Comes As a Choice.* Nashville: Abingdon Press, 1967.

Smith, Asbury. *The Twelve Christ Chose.* New York: Harper & Brothers, 1958.

Smith, Roy L. *Tales I Have Told Twice.* Nashville: Abingdon Press, 1964.

Steimle, Dr. Edmund. "No Proxies." *The Art of Living,* presentation of NBC 4(1960)26.

Stickley, John L. "Christians Anonymous." *The Lion* 1(1965)42.

Strobe, Donald B. "The Hard Sayings of Jesus." *Pulpit Digest* 4(1961)36.

Tittle, Ernest Freemont. *The Lord's Prayer.* Nashville: Abingdon Press, 1952.

Wallis, Charles L. *Notable Sermons from Protestant Pulpits.* Nashville: Abingdon Press, 1958.

Wallis, Charles L. *A Treasury of Sermon Illustrations.* Nashville: Abingdon Press, 1950.

Webb, Lance. "An Honest Skeptic." Sermon preached at North Broadway Methodist Church, 15 February 1959, at Columbus, Ohio. Mimeographed.

Webb, Lance. "I Was Just an Ordinary Man." Sermon preached at North Broadway Methodist Church, 23 September 1958, at Columbus, Ohio. Mimeographed.

Webb, Lance. "Patriotism, Politics and Christian Love." Sermon preached at North Broadway Methodist Church, 9 November 1958, at Columbus, Ohio. Mimeographed.

White, Arthur F. "Those Who Are No People." *Pulpit Digest* 3(1967)50.

Word, Carroll E. "What Is the Goal of Life?" *Pulpit Digest* 3(1963)34.